A JUMPIN' JIM'S UKULELE SONGBOOK

The DAILY UKULELE

365 Songs For Better Living

COMPILED AND ARRANGED BY
LIZ AND JIM BELOFF

7777 W. BLUEMOUND RD. P.O. BOX 13819 MILWAUKEE, WI 53213

Edited by Ronny S. Schiff
Cover and Art Direction by Elizabeth Maihock Beloff
Graphics and Music Typography by Charylu Roberts
Illustrations by Pete McDonnell

Contents

Foreword

Along with an apple a day, a daily allowance of vitamins and minerals and a daily constitutional…playing music regularly is one of the healthiest lifestyle habits you can practice. It makes you smarter. It makes you laugh. And it even has romantic advantages. For those of you who have played a musical instrument, or total beginners who have always longed to play, this book, along with a ukulele, is your key to musical health and happiness. In *The Daily Ukulele* you'll find easy arrangements of hundreds of great, time-tested tunes at your fingertips.

One thing we've learned in all of our years of publishing ukulele songbooks is that the uke is a very social musical instrument. This would explain the recent growth of ukulele clubs throughout the United States and the rest of the world. It's a good bet that at any given moment somewhere on the planet a group of players is gathered together having a great time strumming and singing a bunch of favorite songs.

Part of this is due to the modest nature of the ukulele. Although the uke has always attracted its fair share of virtuosos, most players are perfectly happy to use it as an accompaniment to a song. And when groups of like-minded strummers gather, it can be a memorable experience. For those who have visited a well-established ukulele club, it can seem like a cross between a secret society gathering and a tent revival. Typically, these clubs create their own culture and traditions with regular meetings, special events and gigs, guest performances, and sometimes even annual festivals. At the center of it all are the songs the members are passionate about playing and singing together.

We created *The Daily Ukulele* with these songs in mind. The idea was to pull together 365 well-known songs with easy arrangements in uke-friendly keys that are especially fun to play and sing with others or on your own. Everything from Stephen Foster to Irving Berlin, The Beatles and Bob Dylan, kids songs, gospel songs, Christmas carols, Broadway and Hollywood tunes and even a couple of tributes to the ukulele. And, all bound together in one convenient volume.

Over the years we've seen many worn copies of our other Jumpin' Jim's songbooks. We take special pride in seeing these especially "loved" copies because they clearly have been enjoyed. Here's hoping that this copy of *The Daily Ukulele* will become just as "loved."

Keep on strummin',

Liz and Jim Beloff
Clinton, CT
2010

www.fleamarketmusic.com
www.thedailyukulele.com

Song Index

Ukulele 101

The songs in this book are arranged for ukuleles in C tuning. In this tuning, the individual strings from the top (closest to your nose) to bottom (closest to your toes) are tuned GCEA. A lot of chords can be made with one or two fingers and many of the songs in this book require six chords or less.

Uke C Tuning

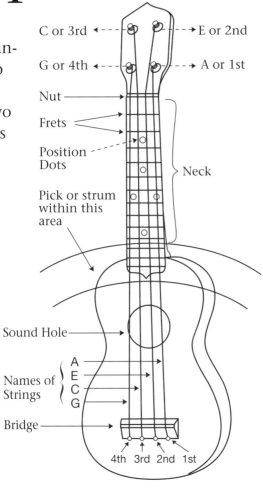

One easy way to tune a ukulele is with a pitchpipe or electronic tuner matching the strings with the notes.

This corresponds to that famous melody:

Here are the notes on the piano:

Keeping In Tune

Most ukuleles have friction tuners that include a small screw at the end of the tuner. The secret to staying in tune is to keep these screws tight enough so that the tuners don't slip, but loose enough that the tuners still turn.

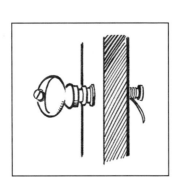

Holding The Uke

Press your uke against your body about 2/3rds of the way up your forearm. Your strumming hand should naturally fall on top of the upper frets (not over the soundhole). Hold the neck of the uke between your thumb and first finger of your other hand, so that your fingers are free to move about the fretboard.

Note: See *Jumpin' Jim's Ukulele Tips 'N' Tunes* if you need a basic ukulele method book.

Making The Chords

1 = Index finger
2 = Second finger
3 = Ring finger
4 = Pinky

You make chords by putting various combinations of fingers on the fretboard. In this songbook you'll find chord diagrams that show where to put your fingers to make the right sound. The vertical lines in the diagrams represent strings and the horizontal lines represent the frets. The numbers at the bottom of the chords shown below indicate what fingers to use.

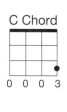

C Chord

0 0 0 3

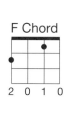

F Chord

2 0 1 0

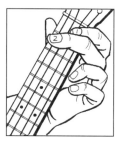

G7 Chord

0 2 1 3

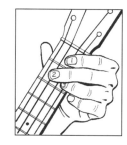

Remember to:

1. When pressing down the strings, use the tips of your fingers.
2. Always press down in the space between the frets, not on them.
3. Press the strings down to the fingerboard. If you hear a buzz it may be because you are not pressing hard enough or are too close to a fret.
4. Keep your thumb at the back of the neck, parallel to the frets.

Making The Strums

The Common Strum: This is the most basic up/down strum. It can be produced solely with your index finger going down the strings with the fingernail and up with the cushion of your fingertip. You can also try this with the pad of your thumb running down the strings and the tip of your index finger going up. This strum will work fine on most of the songs in this book. A good example would be "King Of The Road."

Waltz Strum: This ¾ rhythm can be produced simply with your thumb or index finger in sets of three down strums. You can use this on ¾ songs like "Are You Lonesome Tonight" and "Around The World."

Island Strum: This lilting, syncopated strum is a combination of quick up and down strums plus a roll. In a typical 4-beat measure it would look like this:

⊓ = downstroke

∨ = upstroke

⊓   *roll* ∨   ∨ ⊓ ∨

One and **Two** and **Three** and **Four** and...

Here's how to make the roll strum.

Play the downstroke with your thumb and the upstroke with your index finger. The roll is made by running the ring, middle and index fingers quickly in succession across the strings. Ideal songs to use this on are "Under The Boardwalk" or "Up On The Roof."

Tremolo: This is used often as an ending flourish for a song. It's produced by running your index finger across the strings rapidly. If you are performing, this will suggest to your audience that you are finishing the song and they should get ready to applaud. Try this at the end of any song where you want a "big finish."

How To Use This Book

The best way to use this songbook is, well, daily. Because there are 365 songs, you can play a different song each day for a whole year. (You get one day off during a leap year!) The songs are not always in strict alphabetical order, so consult the index in front when in doubt. We did create two special sections: The first is "Songs For Holidays And Celebrations," where you'll find Christmas carols and other holiday-related material. This section is organized around the calendar year starting with "Auld Lang Syne" for New Year's Eve. The other special section is "Songs For Children" which are tunes that are appropriate for kids to play or parents who want to play for their children.

Many of the songs included here should be easy for you to play and sing right away. Here are a few things to note that will make this songbook especially enjoyable:

1. **Chord Grids**: Just in case you need a reminder of how to make a certain chord, the chord grids for each song are directly under the title, in order of their appearance. The Chord Chart on page 12 shows suggested fingerings.

2. **First Note**: This shows the first singing note of the song. Keep in mind that the lowest note on a GCEA-tuned "my dog has fleas" uke is middle C. As a result, when the first note of a song is below middle C (for example the B in "Are You Lonesome Tonight") the note shown is actually an octave above. Sing that note and then find the octave below.

3. **Instrumentals**: There are a few songs included here that have instrumental sections built into the arrangement. An example of this is in "How Sweet It Is." You are welcome to ignore these sections entirely or take a real solo. Often solo uke performers will make a trumpet or trombone sound with their mouths. Harmonicas and kazoos will work here, too.

4. **N.C.**: Whenever you see N.C. above the staff that means "no chord," a place in the song where you should stop playing until you get to the next chord. This "break" can be a nice flourish that will add drama to your performance. A well-known example is in the sixth line of "Five Foot Two, Eyes Of Blue."

There are some additional symbols that you'll see used throughout the arrangements in this songbook. We've listed a few below with their meanings:

‖: :‖ **Repeat Signs**: These mean that the section within the signs should be performed again before going on to the next section.

1.⌐ ¬ **First Ending**: Play through the measures under this bracketed area and then go back to the beginning of that section. Then look for further endings.

D.C. **Da Capo**: This means "from the beginning." Go back to the beginning of the music.

D.S. **Dal Segno**: Means to look for the 𝄋 sign and repeat that section from the sign.

⊕ **Coda**: Ending section. When you see *"To Coda ⊕"* jump ahead to the closing section that begins with this symbol

The Arrangements

Over the years of publishing our Jumpin' Jim's songbooks, we've fine-tuned our approach to arranging songs for the ukulele. Often it's a careful balancing act between finding a uke-friendly playing key while also keeping the melody in a comfortable singing range. For *The Daily Ukulele* we had an additional goal of keeping the arrangements as streamlined as possible.

The most uke-friendly playing keys for ukuleles in C tuning (GCEA) are C, F, G, D and A, with C and G being the easiest. For a mixed audience of male and female voices of all ages, we try to keep the melodies between G below middle C and C above middle C. That means that the melody in many cases can include single notes that are too low to be picked on a re-entrant, high G, "my dog has fleas" ukulele. For those who want to pick those lower notes, a C-tuned uke with a lowered G string will do the trick.

Transposing

Hopefully, most of the songs in this book are in keys that are easy for you to play and sing. In case a particular song feels too high or too low, you have the option of transposing it to a more comfortable key. If the song is in G and it feels a little high, try dropping the song one whole step down to F. That should be fairly easy to do, since every chord in the arrangement comes down one whole step. G drops to F, C drops to B♭ and D7 drops to C7 and so on. If the song is in F and feels a bit low try going up to G and raising the chords a whole step. With a bit of experience, you should be able to do this in real time, as you are playing the song in tempo. The same would apply for transposing songs from A to G and D to C. If the song still feels too high or low, you may want to try a more dramatic transposition, like G to C or F to C and vice versa.

With some experience you'll become very familiar with the chords that typically appear in uke-friendly keys and will be transposing easily and quickly from one key to the next. This is especially true for simpler songs with a minimum of chords like blues and many kids' and folk tunes. The transposing chart below will help you keep track of the essential chords in the most uke-friendly keys:

Chords in	C	C	F	G7	Am	Dm	E7
	D	D	G	A7	Bm	Em	F♯7
	F	F	B♭	C7	Dm	Gm	A7
	G	G	C	D7	Em	Am	B7
	A	A	D	E7	F♯m	Bm	C♯7

For example, if you wish to transpose a song in the key of C to the key of D, you would

	The Original Chord		The New Chord
Change	C	to	D
Change	F	to	G
Change	G7	to	A7
Change	Am	to	Bm
Change	Dm	to	Em
Change	E7	to	F♯7

In this case, everything moves up one whole step.

Some Chord Alternatives and Shortcuts

Hawaiian D7

The traditional D7 is made by placing your index finger (or middle finger) across all four strings of the second fret and then putting your middle finger (or ring finger) on the third fret of the A string. There is an alternative D7 that is made by putting your middle finger on the second fret of the G string and ring finger on the second fret of the E string. Because this chord form is popular in Hawaii, it is often known as the Hawaiian D7. Besides being easier to play, this D7 has a more open and mellower sound. Part of that is due to the fact that there is no D note in the chord. While either D7 form is fine, we've come to prefer the Hawaiian version and you'll see it used throughout this book.

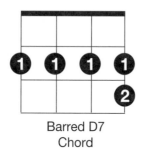

Barred D7
Chord

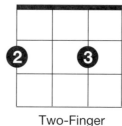

Two-Finger
"Hawaiian" D7 Chord

The Challenging B♭ Chord

For new players, the B♭ is one of the more challenging chords to make on a ukulele. Typically, most players make a B♭ by holding down the first frets of both the A and E string with your index finger and then putting your middle finger on the second fret of the C string and ring finger on the third fret of the G string. A stronger squeeze between your fingers and your thumb is recommended to make a clean-sounding B♭ (no string buzz).

One alternative is to barre the chord. This means laying down your index finger across all the strings on the first fret while adding the middle and ring finger as previously described. For some, stretching the index finger across four strings is easier than holding down two strings with the first joint. (It's also good to practice making these barre chords as often as possible, since they will open up numerous chord possibilities further up the fretboard.) Another even simpler solution is to play the B♭, but leave the top G string open so that it looks like your playing a Gm7. Not having to stretch your hand to the G string makes the chord easier to produce. However, you need to be careful not to strum the G string, only the top three strings. If you accidentally strum the G string, the chord will sound odd, not like a B♭! This alternative is especially appropriate when you just need to play a B♭ for only a brief time (a measure or less).

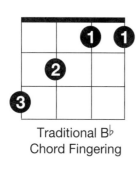

Traditional B♭
Chord Fingering

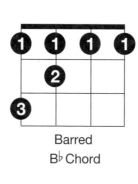

Barred
B♭ Chord

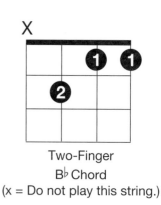

Two-Finger
B♭ Chord
(x = Do not play this string.)

The Dramatic Diminished Chord

You'll find a lot of diminished chords in this book. Most can be found in the older Tin-Pan-Alley songs like "For Me And My Gal." These chords do have a unique, dramatic personality and are especially prominent in the soundtracks of early black and white short films. Most players use all four fingers to make these chords, but they can be barred as well. If you barre the chord with your index finger, you can use your middle and ring finger to cover the remaining notes and thus avoid using your little finger. Another easier option is to play a G7 shape in the same place that calls for a four-finger diminished. As long as you only strum the top three strings, it will sound okay, especially if you're only using the chord for a measure or less.

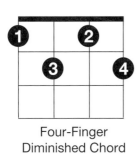

Four-Finger
Diminished Chord

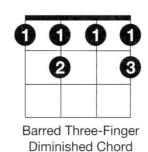

Barred Three-Finger
Diminished Chord

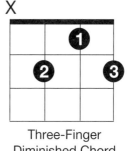

Three-Finger
Diminished Chord
(x = Do not play this string.)

The Pinky G

Most ukulele instruction books recommend playing a G chord with the index, middle and ring fingers. This allows the new player to avoid having to use their weakest finger, the pinky. This is okay to start playing quickly, but it's not very efficient when moving from a G chord to a G7, which is a common transition. In order to do that, all three fingers need to lift and regroup to make the G7. If, on the other hand, the G is made with the middle finger on the second fret of the C string, the ring finger on the second fret of the A string and pinky on the third fret of the E string you need only lift the pinky and place the index finger on the first fret of the E string to make the same transition.

There are other advantages to playing a G chord with your little finger. For example, look at how easily you can make a first position E7 coming from a pinky G in the arrangement of "Are You Lonesome Tonight." Fingered correctly, many of the chords in that song will fall into each other naturally. In fact, over time you may realize that you're making your first position C chord with your pinky because it frees up the three other fingers to plop down on a variety of follow-up chords. And, keep in mind that the sooner you're able to use your pinky, the sooner you can start using those rich, jazzy and nuanced 4-finger chords that the master players employ. It's helpful to think of this fingering as part of the overall art of moving from chord to chord. Ultimately it is the ease with which you can move from one chord to the next that will accelerate your progress.

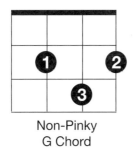

Non-Pinky
G Chord

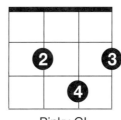

Pinky G!

Chord Chart

Tune Ukulele
G   C   E   A

Major Chords

A | A♯ / B♭ | B | C | C♯ / D♭ | D | D♯ / E♭ | E | F | F♯ / G♭ | G | G♯ / A♭

Minor Chords

Am | A♯m / B♭m | Bm | Cm | C♯m / D♭m | Dm | D♯m / E♭m | Em | Fm | F♯m / G♭m | Gm | G♯m / A♭m

Dominant Seventh Chords

A⁷ | A♯⁷ / B♭⁷ | B⁷ | C⁷ | C♯⁷ / D♭⁷ | D⁷ | D♯⁷ / E♭⁷ | E⁷ | F⁷ | F♯⁷ / G♭⁷ | G⁷ | G♯⁷ / A♭⁷

Minor Seventh Chords

Am⁷ | A♯m⁷ / B♭m⁷ | Bm⁷ | Cm⁷ | C♯m⁷ / D♭m⁷ | Dm⁷ | D♯m⁷ / E♭m⁷ | Em⁷ | Fm⁷ | F♯m⁷ / G♭m⁷ | Gm⁷ | G♯m⁷ / A♭m⁷

Major Sixth Chords

A⁶ | A♯⁶ / B♭⁶ | B⁶ | C⁶ | C♯⁶ / D♭⁶ | D⁶ | D♯⁶ / E♭⁶ | E⁶ | F⁶ | F♯⁶ / G♭⁶ | G⁶ | G♯⁶ / A♭⁶

Minor Sixth Chords

Am⁶ | A♯m⁶ / B♭m⁶ | Bm⁶ | Cm⁶ | C♯m⁶ / D♭m⁶ | Dm⁶ | D♯m⁶ / E♭m⁶ | Em⁶ | Fm⁶ | F♯m⁶ / G♭m⁶ | Gm⁶ | G♯m⁶ / A♭m⁶

Major Seventh Chords

Amaj⁷ | A♯maj⁷ / B♭maj⁷ | Bmaj⁷ | Cmaj⁷ | C♯maj⁷ / D♭maj⁷ | Dmaj⁷ | D♯maj⁷ / E♭maj⁷ | Emaj⁷ | Fmaj⁷ | F♯maj⁷ / G♭maj⁷ | Gmaj⁷ | G♯maj⁷ / A♭maj⁷

Augmented Fifth Chords (+ or aug)

A+ | A♯+ / B♭+ | B+ | C+ | C♯+ / D♭+ | D+ | D♯+ / E♭+ | E+ | F+ | F♯+ / G♭+ | G+ | G♯+ / A♭+

Diminished Seventh Chords (dim)

Adim | A♯dim / B♭dim | Bdim | Cdim | C♯dim / D♭dim | Ddim | D♯dim / E♭dim | Edim | Fdim | F♯dim / G♭dim | Gdim | G♯dim / A♭dim

Are You Lonesome Tonight?

Words and Music by
ROY TURK and LOU HANDMAN

Are you lone - some to - night, do you miss me to - night? Are you sor - ry we drift - ed a - part? Does your mem - o - ry stray to a bright sum - mer day, when I kissed you and called you sweet - heart? Do the chairs in your par - lor seem emp - ty and bare? Do you gaze at your door - step and pic - ture me there? Is your heart filled with pain, shall I come back a - gain? Tell me, dear, are you lone - some to - night?

After You've Gone

Ain't Misbehavin'

Words by
ANDY RAZAF

Music by THOMAS "FATS" WALLER
and HARRY BROOKS

1. No one to talk with, all by my-self, no one to walk with, but
2. I know for cer-tain the one I love, I'm through with flirt-in', it's
3. I don't stay out late, don't care to go, I'm home a-bout eight, just

I'm hap-py on__ the shelf; ain't mis-be-hav-in', I'm sav-in' my love for you.__
just you I'm think-in' of; ain't mis-be-hav-in', I'm sav-in' my love for
me and my ra-di-o; ain't mis-be-hav-in', I'm sav-in' my love for

you.__ you. Like Jack Hor-ner in the cor-ner, don't go no-where,

what do I care? Your kiss-es are worth wait-in' for, be-lieve me.

Ain't She Sweet

Words by
JACK YELLEN

Music by
MILTON AGER

FIRST NOTE

Jauntily

1. Ain't she sweet? See her com-ing down the street! Now I ask you ver-y
2. Ain't she nice? Look her o-ver once or twice.

con-fi-den-tial-ly, ain't she sweet?

nice? Just cast an eye_____ in her di-rec-tion.___

___ Oh, me! Oh, my!_____ Ain't that per-fec-tion?_____ I re-peat, don't you

think that's kind of neat? And I ask you ver-y con-fi-den-tial-ly, ain't she sweet?___

Ain't We Got Fun?

Words by GUS KAHN
and RAYMOND B. EGAN

Music by
RICHARD A. WHITING

All I Have To Do Is Dream

All My Loving

Words and Music by
JOHN LENNON and PAUL McCARTNEY

All Of Me

Words and Music by
SEYMOUR SIMONS
and GERALD MARKS

Aloha 'Oe

Words and Music by
QUEEN LILIUOKALANI

A - lo - ha 'oe, a - lo - ha 'oe, e - ke o - na - o - na
Fare - well to thee, fare - well to thee, thou__ charm - ing one who

no - ho i - ka li - po. One fond em - brace a ho - 'i - a - 'e
dwells a - mong the bow - ers. One fond em - brace be - fore I now de -

au, un - til we meet__ a - gain.__
part, un - til we meet__ a - gain.__

Amazing Grace

Words by
JOHN NEWTON

Traditional Melody

1. A - maz - ing grace, how sweet the sound that saved a
grace that taught my heart to fear and grace my

wretch like me!__ I once was lost, but now am
fears re - lieved;__ how pre - cious did that grace ap -

found, was blind, but now I see.__ 2. 'Twas
pear, the hour I first be - lieved.__ 3. Through

Additional Lyrics

3. Through many dangers, toils, and snares
   I have already come;
   'twas grace that brought me safe thus far,
   and grace will lead me home.

4. When we've been there ten thousand years,
   bright shining as the sun,
   we've no less days to sing God's praise,
   than when we first begun.

Always

Words and Music by
IRVING BERLIN

I'll be lov-ing you, al-ways_____ with a love that's true,

al-ways._____ When the things you've planned need a help-ing hand,

I will un-der-stand, al-ways al-ways. Days may not be fair,

al-ways._____ That's when I'll be there, al-ways._____ Not for just an

hour, not for just a day, not for just a year, but al-ways._____

America, The Beautiful

Words by
KATHERINE LEE BATES

Music by
SAMUEL A. WARD

America
(My Country 'Tis Of Thee)

Words by
SAMUEL FRANCIS SMITH

Music from
THESAURUS MUSICUS

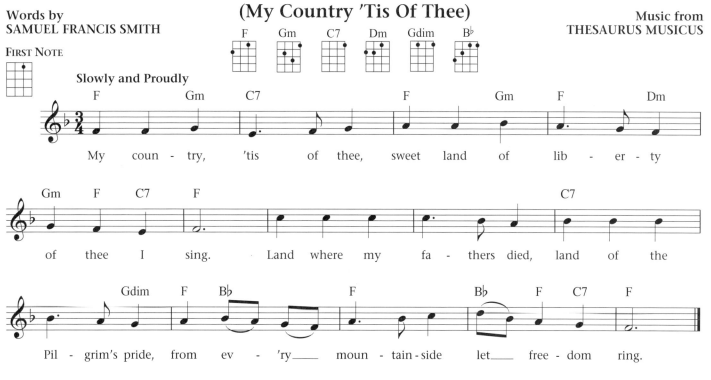

Anchors Aweigh

**Words by ALFRED HART MILES
and ROYAL LOVELL
Additional Lyric by
GEORGE D. LOTTMAN**

Music by
CHARLES A. ZIMMERMAN

Spirited March

Stand Na-vy out to sea, fight our bat-tle cry;

we'll nev-er change our course, so vi-cious foe steer shy-y-y-y.

Roll out the T. N. T. an-chors a-weigh.____ Sail on to

vic-to-ry and sink their bones to Da-vy Jones hoo-ray!____

Any Time

Words and Music by
HERBERT HAPPY LAWSON

Around The World

Words and Music by VICTOR YOUNG
and HAROLD ADAMSON

FIRST NOTE

Slow waltz tempo

A - round the world I've searched for you, I trav-eled on, when hope was gone, to keep a

ren - dez - vous. I knew some - where, some - time, some - how, you'd look at

me, and I would see the smile you're smil - ing now. It might have been in Coun - ty

Down, or in New York, in gay Pa - ree, or e - ven Lon - don Town. No more will

I go all a - round the world, for I have found my world in you.____

Avalon

Words by
AL JOLSON and B.G. DeSYLVA

Music by
VINCENT ROSE

Baby Love

Words and Music by
BRIAN HOLLAND, EDWARD HOLLAND
and LAMONT DOZIER

Baby, Won't You Please Come Home

Words and Music by CHARLES WARFIELD
and CLARENCE WILLIAMS

Bad, Bad Leroy Brown

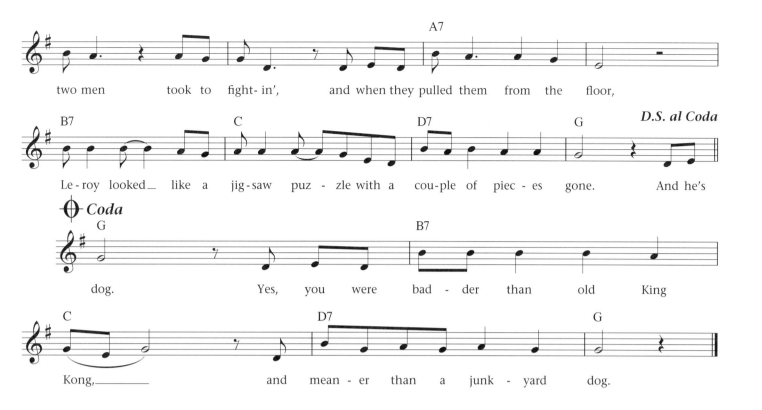

two men took to fight- in', and when they pulled them from the floor,

Le- roy looked_ like a jig-saw puz- zle with a cou-ple of piec- es gone. And he's

dog. Yes, you were bad- der than old King

Kong,_____ and mean- er than a junk- yard dog.

Baby Face

Words and Music by
BENNY DAVIS and HARRY AKST

Ba - by face,_____ you've got the cut- est lit- tle ba - by face,_____

there's not an- oth- er one could take your place.___ Ba - by face,_____

my poor heart___ is jump- in'; you sure have start- ed some- thin'. Ba - by face,_____

I'm up in heav- en when I'm in your fond em- brace._____ I did- n't need a shove,_

_ 'cause I just fell in love___ with your pret- ty ba- by face._____

The Battle Hymn Of The Republic

Words by
JULIA WARD HOWE

Music by
WILLIAM STEFFE

Beautiful Dreamer

Words and Music by
STEPHEN FOSTER

Beautiful Brown Eyes

D   G   A7

Traditional

FIRST NOTE

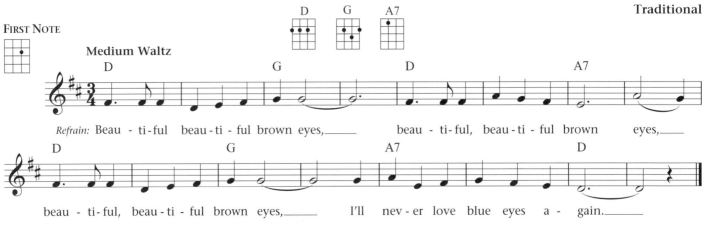

Medium Waltz

Refrain: Beau-ti-ful beau-ti-ful brown eyes,____ beau-ti-ful, beau-ti-ful brown eyes,

beau-ti-ful, beau-ti-ful brown eyes,____ I'll nev-er love blue eyes a-gain.

Additional Lyrics

1. Willie, my darling, I love you,
   love you with all of my heart.
   Tomorrow we might have been married,
   but drinkin' has kept us apart.
   Refrain

2. Down to the barroom he staggered;
   staggered and fell at the door.
   The very last words he uttered:
   "I'll never get drunk any more."
   Refrain

3. Seven long years I've been married.
   I wish I was single again.
   A woman never knows of her troubles
   until she has married a man.
   Refrain

The Best Things In Life Are Free

**Words and Music by
B.G. DeSYLVA, LEW BROWN,
and RAY HENDERSON**

FIRST NOTE

Brightly

The moon be-longs to ev-'ry-one,____ the best things in life are

free.____ The stars be-long to ev-'ry-one,____ they gleam there for

you and me.____ The flow-ers in spring,____ the rob-ins that sing,_

_ the sun-beams that shine,____ they're yours, they're mine! And love can

come to ev-'ry-one;____ the best things in life are free.____

Bill Bailey, Won't You Please Come Home

Words and Music by
HUGHIE CANNON

Blowin' In The Wind

Words and Music by
BOB DYLAN

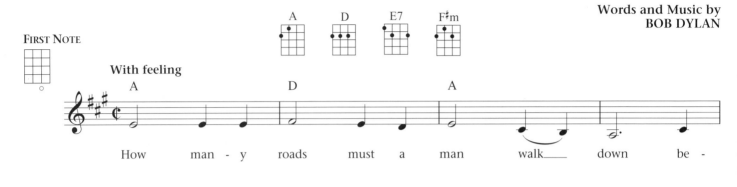

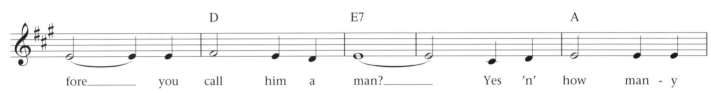

How man-y roads must a man walk___ down be-

fore___ you call him a man?___ Yes 'n' how man-y

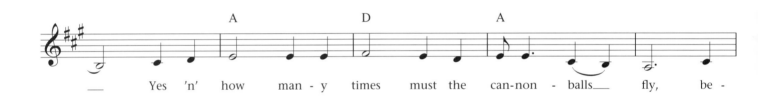

seas must the white dove___ sail, be - fore___ she sleeps in the sand?___

___ Yes 'n' how man-y times must the can-non - balls___ fly, be -

fore they're for - ev - er banned?___ The ans - wer, my friend, is

blow-in' in the wind, the ans - wer is blow-in' in the wind.___

Additional Lyrics

2. How many times must a man look up, before he can see the sky?
   Yes 'n' how many ears must one man have, before he can hear people cry?
   Yes 'n' how many deaths will it take 'til he knows, that too many people have died?
   The answer, my friend, is blowin' in the wind, the answer is blowin' in the wind.

3. How many years can a mountain exist, before it is washed to the sea?
   Yes 'n' how many years can some people exist, before they're allowed to be free?
   Yes 'n' how many times can a man turn his head, pretending that he just doesn't see?
   The answer, my friend, is blowin' in the wind, the answer is blowin' in the wind.

Blue Hawaii

Words and Music by LEO ROBIN
and RALPH RAINGER

Blue Skies

Words and Music by
IRVING BERLIN

1. Blue skies smil-ing at me, noth-ing but
2. Blue-birds sing-ing a song, noth-ing but
3. Blue days all of them gone, noth-ing but

blue skies do I see.
blue-birds from now on.
blue skies from now on.

Nev-er saw the sun shin-ing so bright, nev-er saw things go-ing so right.

D.C. al Fine

No-tic-ing the days hur-ry-ing by, when you're in love my how they fly.

Bye Bye Blues

Words and Music by
FRED HAMM, DAVE BENNETT,
BERT LOWN and CHAUNCEY GRAY

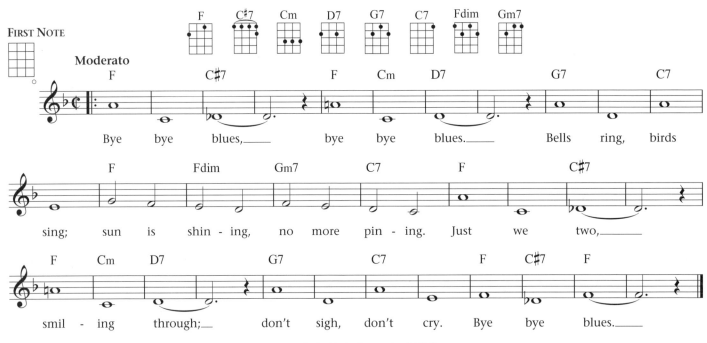

Bye bye blues, bye bye blues. Bells ring, birds

sing; sun is shin-ing, no more pin-ing. Just we two,

smil-ing through; don't sigh, don't cry. Bye bye blues.

Brown Eyed Girl

Words and Music by
VAN MORRISON

Additional Lyrics

2. Whatever happened to Tuesday and so slow
going down the old mine with a transistor radio.
Standing in the sunlight laughing,
hiding behind a rainbow's wall.
Slipping and a-sliding,
all along the waterfall
with you, my brown eyed girl,
you, my brown eyed girl.
Do you remember when we used to sing:
Chorus

3. So hard to find my way, now that I'm all on my own.
I saw you just the other day, my, how you have grown.
Cast my memory back there, Lord;
sometime I'm overcome thinking 'bout
making love in the green grass
behind the stadium,
with you, my brown eyed girl,
with you, my brown eyed girl.
Do you remember when we used to sing:
Chorus

Buffalo Gals (Won't You Come Out Tonight)

Words and Music by
COOL WHITE (JOHN HODGES)

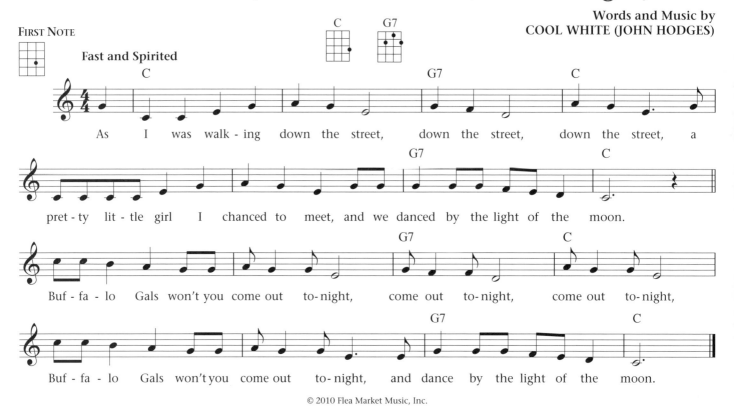

Fast and Spirited

As I was walk-ing down the street, down the street, down the street, a pret-ty lit-tle girl I chanced to meet, and we danced by the light of the moon.

Buf-fa-lo Gals won't you come out to-night, come out to-night, come out to-night,

Buf-fa-lo Gals won't you come out to-night, and dance by the light of the moon.

Bye Bye Blackbird

Words by
MORT DIXON

Music by
RAY HENDERSON

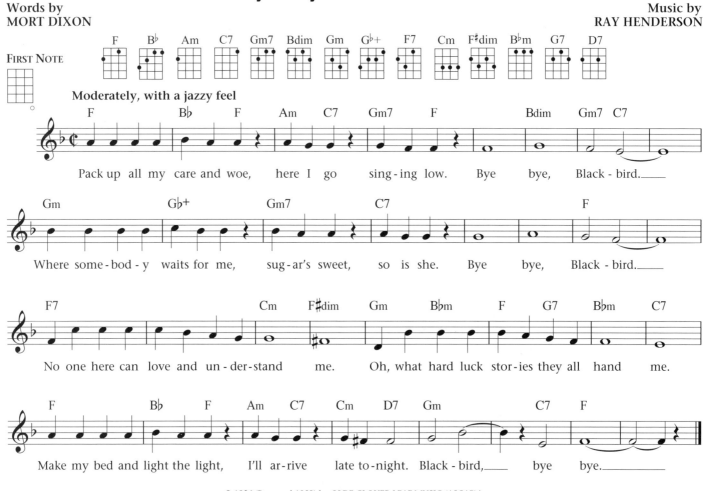

Moderately, with a jazzy feel

Pack up all my care and woe, here I go sing-ing low. Bye bye, Black-bird.___

Where some-bod-y waits for me, sug-ar's sweet, so is she. Bye bye, Black-bird.___

No one here can love and un-der-stand me. Oh, what hard luck stor-ies they all hand me.

Make my bed and light the light, I'll ar-rive late to-night. Black-bird,___ bye bye.___

Bye Bye Love

Words and Music by FELICE BRYANT
and BOUDLEAUX BRYANT

1. There goes my ba — by___ with some - one new;
2. I'm through with ro - mance, I'm through with love;

___ she sure looks hap - py___ I sure am blue.
___ I'm through with count - ing,___ the stars a - bove.

___ She was my ba - by,___ 'til he stepped in.
___ And here's the rea - son___ that I'm so free:

___ Good - bye to ro - mance___ that might have been.
___ my lov - in' ba - by___ is through with me.

Bye bye, love, bye bye, hap - pi - ness,___ hel - lo

lone - li - ness, I think I'm gon - na cry.___ Bye bye, love,

bye bye, sweet ca - ress;___ hel - lo emp - ti - ness;___ I

1. 2.

feel like I could die.___ Bye bye, my love, bye bye. bye.

By The Beautiful Sea

Words by
HAROLD R. ATTERIDGE

Music by
HARRY CARROLL

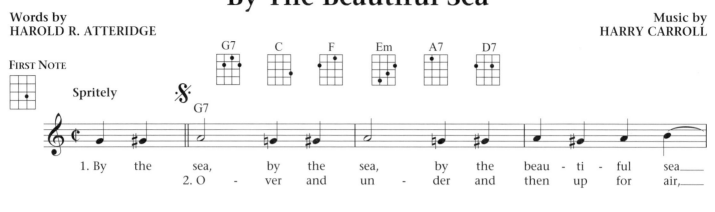

FIRST NOTE

Spritely

1. By the sea, by the sea, by the beau - ti - ful sea___
2. O - ver and un - der and then up for air,___

___ you and I, you and I, oh how
___ Pa is rich, Ma is rich, so now

hap - py we'll be.___ When each wave comes a -
what do we care?___

roll - ing in, we will duck or

swim, and we'll float and fool a - round the wa - ter.

I love to be be - side your side, be - side the sea, be - side the

sea - side,___ by the beau - ti - ful sea.___

By The Light Of The Silvery Moon

Words by
ED MADDE

Music by
GUS EDWARDS

By the light___ of the sil - ver - y moon,___ I want to spoon,___ to my hon - ey I'll croon love's tune. Hon - ey- moon___ __ keep a - shin - ing in June,___ your sil - v'ry beams will bring love dreams, we'll be cud - dling soon,___ by the sil - ver - y moon.___

Come And Go With Me

Spiritual

Come and go with me to that land, come and go with me to that land, come and go with me to that land where I'm bound.___ __ Come and go with me to that land, come and go with me to that land, come and go with me to that land where I'm bound.

Additional Lyrics

2. There will be freedom in that land...
3. There will be singing in that land...
4. There will be peace in that land...
5. Come and go with me to that land...

Cabaret

Words by
FRED EBB

Music by
JOHN KANDER

1. What good is sit-ting a-lone in your room?___ Come hear the mu - sic
2. Put down the knit-ting, the book and the broom,___ time for a hol - i -
3. No use per-mit-ing some proph - et of doom___ to wipe ev - 'ry smile a -
4. Start by ad-mit-ing from cra - dle to tomb,___ it is - n't that long a

play;___
day;___
way;___
stay;___

life is a cab - a - ret old chum,___ come to the

cab - a - ret.___

ret. Come taste the wine. Come hear the band.

Come blow the horn, start cel - e - brat - ing, right this way, your ta - ble's wait - ing.

ret, old chum,___ come to the cab - a - ret.___

The Caissons Go Rolling Along

Words and Music by
EDMUND L. GRUBER

FIRST NOTE

With movement

C

1. O - ver hill, o - ver dale, as we hit the dust - y
2. 'Til our fin - al ride, it will al - ways be our

G7   C

trail, and the Cais - sons go roll - ing a - long.
pride to keep those Cais - sons a - roll - ing a - long.   In and

out, hear them shout: "Coun - ter march right a - bout" and the

G7   C   G7   C

Cais - sons go roll - ing a - long.   For it's hi! hi!

Am   F   C   Am   D7

hee! In the field ar - til - ler - y, shout out your num - bers loud and

G   G7   C   E7   F

strong.   For wher - e'er you go, you will al - ways

C   G7   C

know that the Cais - sons go roll - ing a - long.

California Dreamin'

California, Here I Come

Words and Music by
AL JOLSON, B.G. DeSYLVA
and JOSEPH MEYER

Cal - i - for - nia, here I come,__ right back where I start-ed from.__

Where bow - ers of flow - ers bloom in the sun.__ Each morn - ing

at dawn - ing, bird - ies sing and ev - 'ry - thing. A sun - kissed miss said,

"Don't be late."__ That's why I can hard - ly wait.__ O - pen

up that Gold-en Gate;__ Cal - i - for - nia, here I come!__

Can't Buy Me Love

Words and Music by
JOHN LENNON and PAUL McCARTNEY

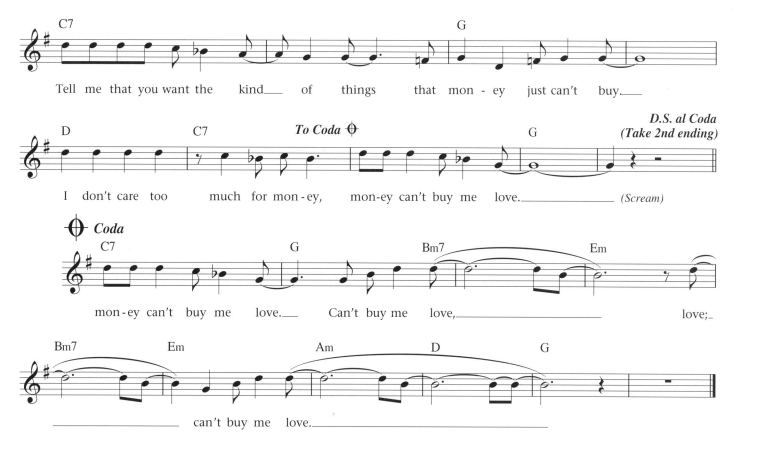

Tell me that you want the kind___ of things that mon-ey just can't buy.___

I don't care too much for mon-ey, mon-ey can't buy me love.___ (Scream)

D.S. al Coda
(Take 2nd ending)

Coda

mon-ey can't buy me love.___ Can't buy me love,___ love;_

can't buy me love.___

Careless Love

Traditional

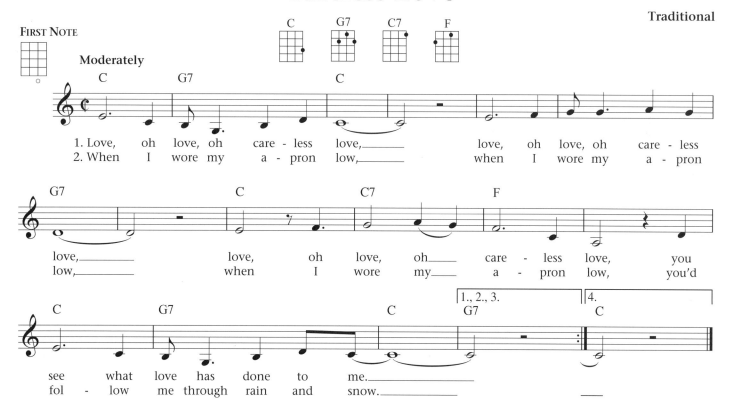

1. Love, oh love, oh care-less love,_____ love, oh love, oh care-less
2. When I wore my a-pron low,_____ when I wore my a-pron

love,_____ love, oh love, oh___ care-less love, you
low,_____ when I wore my___ a-pron low, you'd

see what love has done to me._____
fol-low me through rain and snow._____

Additional Lyrics

3. Now my apron strings don't pin.
   Now my apron strings don't pin.
   Now my apron strings don't pin.
   You pass my door and you don't come in.

4. I cried last night and the night before.
   I cried last night and the night before.
   I cried last night and the night before.
   Gonna cry tonight and cry no more.

49

Can't Help But Smile

Words and Music by
JIM BELOFF

Can't Help Falling In Love

Words and Music by
GEORGE DAVID WEISS,
HUGO PERETTI and
LUIGI CREATORE

Wise men say on-ly fools rush in,____ but I can't help fall-ing in
Shall I stay? Would it be a sin?____ If I can't help fall-ing in

love with you.
love with you.
Like a ri-ver flows sure-ly to the sea, dar-ling so it goes,

some things__ are meant to be. Take my hand, take my whole life too,____ for I can't

help fall-ing in love with you,____ for I can't help fall-ing in love with you.

Clementine

Words and Music by
PERCY MONTROSE

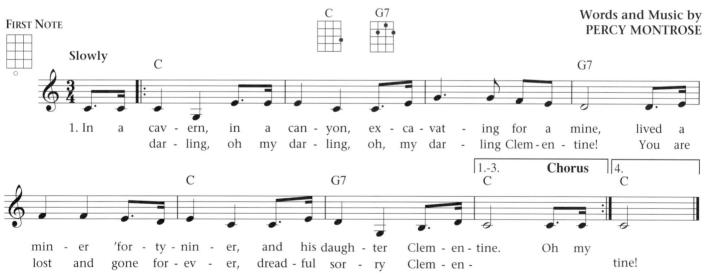

1. In a cav-ern, in a can-yon, ex-ca-vat-ing for a mine, lived a
   dar-ling, oh my dar-ling, oh, my dar-ling Clem-en-tine! You are

1.-3. **Chorus** **4.**

min-er 'for-ty-nin-er, and his daugh-ter Clem-en-tine. Oh my
lost and gone for-ev-er, dread-ful sor-ry Clem-en-   tine!

Additional Lyrics

2. Light she was and, like a fairy,
   and her shoes were number nine;
   herring boxes, without topses,
   sandals were for Clementine.
   Chorus

3. Drove she ducklings to the water,
   every morning just at nine;
   hit her foot against a splinter,
   fell into the foaming brine.
   Chorus

4. Ruby lips above the water
   blowing bubbles soft and fine;
   but alas I was no swimmer,
   so I lost my Clementine.
   Chorus

Carolina In The Morning

Chapel Of Love

Words and Music by PHIL SPECTOR,
ELLIE GREENWICH, and JEFF BARRY

Chicago
(That Toddlin' Town)

Words and Music by
FRED FISHER

FIRST NOTE

Medium bounce

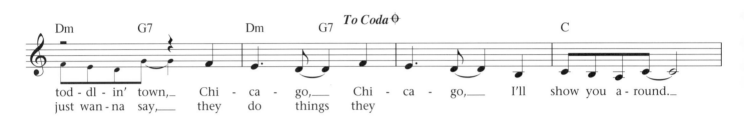

1. Chi - ca - go,___ Chi - ca - go,___ that tod - dl - in' town,

State Street,_ that great street,_ I just wan - na say,___

tod - dl - in' town,_ Chi - ca - go,___ Chi - ca - go,___ I'll show you a - round._

just wan - na say,___ they do things they

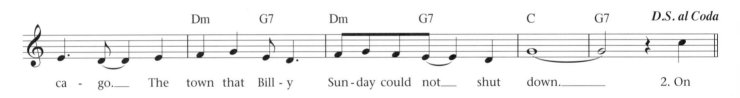

I love it! Bet your bot - tom dol - lar you'll lose the blues_ in Chi - ca - go,___ Chi -

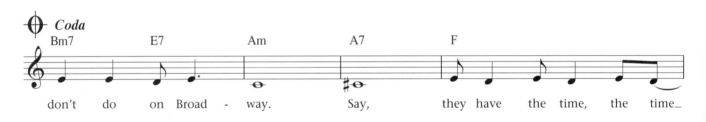

ca - go.___ The town that Bill - y Sun - day could not___ shut down.___ 2. On

Coda

don't do on Broad - way. Say, they have the time, the time_

___ of their life. I saw a man and he danced with his wife in Chi -

ca - go,___ Chi - ca - go, my home - town.___

Chinatown, My Chinatown

Words by
WILLIAM JEROME

Music by
JEAN SCHWARTZ

FIRST NOTE

Briskly

Chi - na - town, my Chi - na - town,__ where the lights are low.__ Hearts that know no

oth - er land,__ drift - ing to and fro.__ Dream - y, dream - y, Chi - na - town,__ al - mond

eyes of brown.__ Hearts seem light and life seems bright__ in dream - y Chi - na - town.__

Cindy

Southern Appalachian Folksong

FIRST NOTE

Lively

You ought to see my Cin - dy, she lives a - way down South, and she's so sweet, the

hon - ey - bees__ swarm a - round her mouth. Get a - long home, Cin - dy, Cin - dy, get a - long

Chorus

home, Cin - dy, Cin - dy, get a - long home, Cin - dy, Cin - dy, I'll mar - ry you some - day.

Additional Lyrics

2. I wish I was an apple,
a-hangin' on the tree,
and every time that Cindy passed,
she'd take a bite of me.
Chorus

3. I wish I had a needle,
as fine as I could sew.
I'd sew that gal to my coattail,
and down the road we'd go.
Chorus

4. Cindy in the springtime,
Cindy in the fall,
if I can't have my Cindy,
I'll have no gal at all.
Chorus

(They Long To Be) Close To You

Lyric by
HAL DAVID

Music by
BURT BACHARACH

Consider Yourself

Words and Music by
LIONEL BART

Crazy

Words and Music by
WILLIE NELSON

Danny Boy

Words by
FREDERICK EDWARD WEATHERLY

Traditional Irish Melody

Daydream

Words and Music by
JOHN SEBASTIAN

1. What a day for a day- dream,___ what a day for a
2. I've been hav-ing a sweet___ dream,___ I've been dream-in' since I

day- dream- in' boy.___ And I'm lost in a day- dream,___
woke up to- day.___ It's star-ring me and my sweet___ dream,___

dream- in' 'bout my bun-dle of joy.___ And e- ven if time ain't real- ly
'cause she's the one makes me feel___ this way.___ And e- ven if time___ is pass-ing

on my side,___ it's one of those days for tak-ing a walk out- side.___
by a lot,___ I could-n't care less a- bout the dues you say I___ got.

I'm blow-ing the day to take a walk in the sun,___
To- mor- row I'll pay the dues for drop- ping my load,___

and fall on my face on some- bod- y's new mown lawn.___
a pie in the face for be- in' a

1.
2. sleep-y bull- toad.___

D.C. al Coda (3rd verse)

Coda

or you may be day- dream- in' for a thou-sand years.___ What a day for a day-

dream,___ cus-tom-made for a day-dream-in' boy.___ And I'm lost in a day-

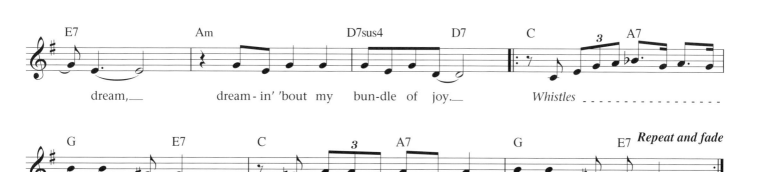

3. *Whistle*
   Whistle
   Whistle
   Whistle
   And you can be sure that if you're feelin' right,
   a daydream will last 'til long into the night.
   Tomorrow at breakfast you may pick up your ears,
   or you may be daydreamin' for a thousand years.

Dinah

Words by
SAM M. LEWIS and JOE YOUNG

Music by
HARRY AKST

Daydream Believer

Words and Music by
JOHN STEWART

Devoted To You

Words and Music by
BOUDLEAUX BRYANT

Deep In The Heart Of Texas

Words by
JUNE HERSHEY

Music by
DON SWANDER

Copyright © 1941 by Melody Lane Publications, Inc.
Copyright Renewed

Dixie Land

Words and Music by
DANIEL D. EMMETT

1. I___ wish I was___ in the land of cot-ton, old times there are not for-got-ten
2. Dix-ie Land___ where___ I was born in, ear-ly on one frost-y morn-in' look a-

way! Look a-way! Look a-way! Dix-ie Land. In___ Land. Then I wish I was in Dix-ie, hoo-

ray! Hoo-ray! In Dix-ie Land, I'll take my stand to live and die in Dix-ie; a-way, a-

way, a-way down south in Dix-ie. A-way, a-way, a-way down south in Dix-ie.

Do Lord

Traditional

I've got a home in glo-ry-land that out-shines the sun, I've got a home in

glo-ry-land that out-shines the sun, I've got a home in glo-ry-land that

out-shines the sun, 'way be-yond___ the blue. Do Lord, oh do Lord, oh

do re-mem-ber me. Oh Lord-y, do Lord, oh do Lord, oh do re-mem-ber me.

Do Lord, oh do Lord, oh do re-mem-ber me, 'way be-yond___ the blue.

Don't Be Cruel (To A Heart That's True)

Words and Music by
OTIS BLACKWELL and ELVIS PRESLEY

of._____ Don't be cruel_____ to a heart that's true._____

Don't be cruel_____ to a heart that's true._____ I don't want no oth - er

love, ba - by, it's just you I'm think - ing of._____

Down By The Riverside

African American Spiritual

FIRST NOTE

With feeling

1. Gon - na lay down my sword and shield_ down by the riv - er - side,_

down by the riv - er - side,_ down by the riv - er - side._ Gon - na lay down my

sword and shield_ down by the riv - er - side,_ and stud - y_____ war no more._____

Chorus

_____ I ain't gon - na stud - y war no more, I ain't gon - na stud - y war no more, I ain't gon - na

stud - y_____ war no more._____ I ain't gon - na more._____

Additional Lyrics

2. I'm gonna join hands with everyone,
   down by the riverside, down by the riverside,
   down by the riverside.
   I'm gonna join hands with everyone,
   down by the riverside,
   and study war no more.
   Chorus

Don't Get Around Much Anymore

Words and Music by
DUKE ELLINGTON and BOB RUSSELL

Down In The Valley

Traditional American Folksong

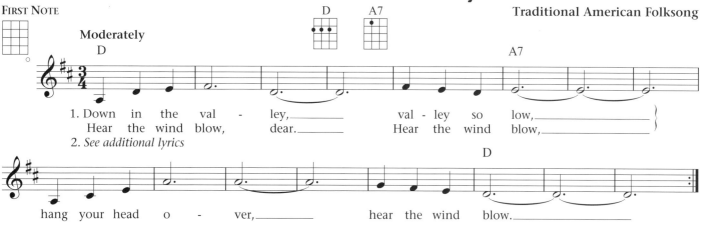

1. Down in the val - ley,_____ val - ley so low,_____
Hear the wind blow, dear._____ Hear the wind blow,
2. *See additional lyrics*

hang your head o - ver,_____ hear the wind blow.

Additional Lyrics

2. Roses love sunshine, violets love dew;
angels in heaven, know I love you.
Know I love you dear, know I love you.
angels in heaven know I love you.

3. Build me a castle forty feet high,
so I can see him as he rides by.
As he rides by love, as he rides by.
So I can see him as he rides by.

4. If you don't love me, love whom you please,
throw your arms 'round me, give my heart ease.
Give my heart ease, love, give my heart ease.
Throw your arms 'round me, give my heart ease.

5. Write me a letter, send it by mail.
Send it in care of Birmingham jail.
Birmingham jail, love, Birmingham jail.
Send it in care of Birmingham jail.

Dream A Little Dream Of Me

Words by GUS KAHN

Music by WILBUR SCHWANDT and FABIAN ANDREE

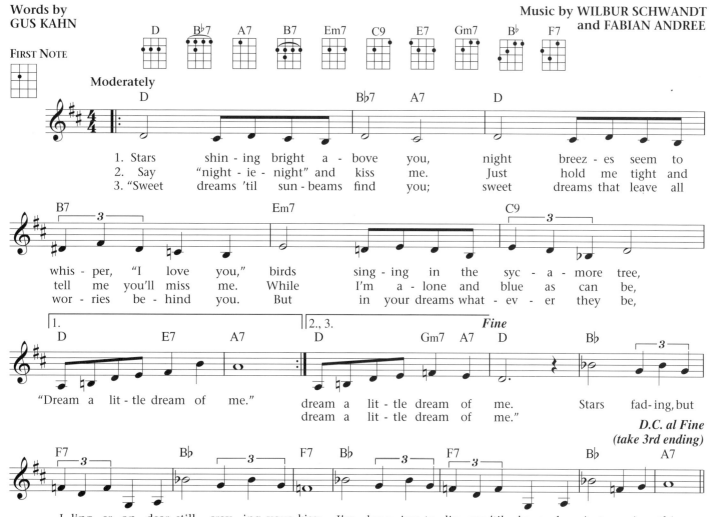

1. Stars shin - ing bright a - bove you, night breez - es seem to
2. Say "night - ie - night" and kiss me. Just hold me tight and
3. "Sweet dreams 'til sun - beams find you; Just sweet dreams that leave all

whis - per, "I love you," birds sing - ing in the syc - a - more tree,
tell me you'll miss me. While I'm a - lone and blue as can be,
wor - ries be - hind you. But in your dreams what - ev - er they be,

"Dream a lit - tle dream of me."
dream a lit - tle dream of me.
dream a lit - tle dream of me." Stars fad - ing, but

I ling - er on, dear, still crav - ing your kiss; I'm long - ing to lin - ger 'til dawn, dear, just say - ing this:

Don't Worry, Be Happy

Words and Music by
BOBBY McFERRIN

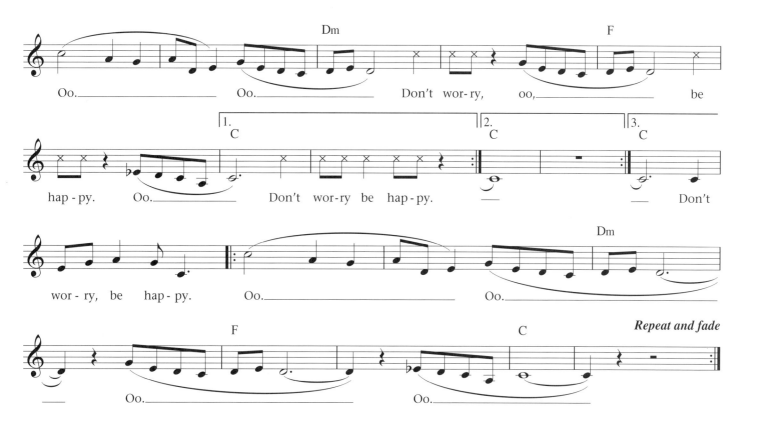

Oo. _____ Oo. _____ Don't wor-ry, oo, _____ be

hap-py. Oo. _____ Don't wor-ry be hap-py. _____ _____ Don't

wor - ry, be hap - py. Oo. _____ Oo. _____

Repeat and fade

_____ Oo. _____ Oo. _____

The Drunken Sailor

Sea Chanty

FIRST NOTE

Rousing

1. Oh, what shall we do with the drunk - en sail - or? What shall we do with the
2. Sling him in the long boat 'til he's so - ber, sling him in the long boat

drunk - en sail - or? What shall we do with the drunk - en sail - or, ⎫
'til he's so - ber, sling him in the long boat 'til he's so - ber, ⎭ ear - lye in the

Chorus

morn - ing? Way, hey and up she ris - es, way, hey and up she ris - es.

Way, hey and up she ris - es, ear - lye in the morn - ing.

Additional Lyrics

3. Give 'im a dose of salt and water,
   give 'im a dose of salt and water,
   give 'im a dose of salt and water
   earlye in the morning.
   Chorus

4. Shave his belly with a rusty razor,
   shave his belly with a rusty razor,
   shave his belly with a rusty razor
   earlye in the morning.
   Chorus

Downtown

Words and Music by
TONY HATCH

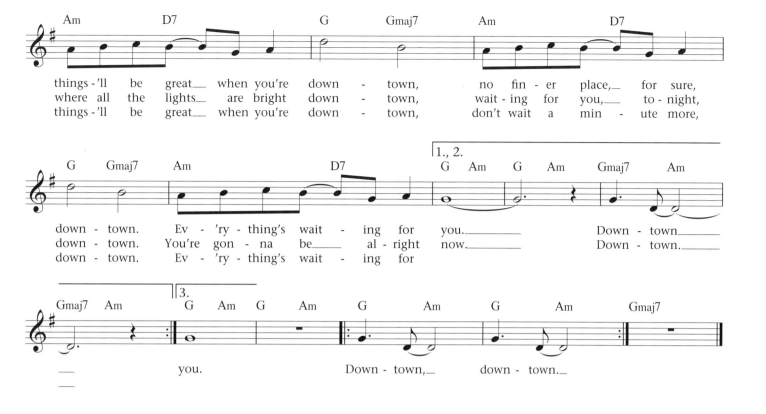

Ev'ry Time I Feel The Spirit

African-American Spiritual

Eight Days A Week

Words and Music by JOHN LENNON
and PAUL McCARTNEY

Brightly, with a swing feel

1. Ooh I need your love, babe, guess you know it's true.___
2. Love you ev-'ry day, girl,___ al-ways on my mind.___

Hope you need my love, babe,___ just like I need you.___
One thing I can say, girl,___ love you all the time.___ Hold me,___

love me.___ Hold me,___ love me.___ I ain't got noth-in' but love, babe,___

eight days a week.___ Eight days a week, I

love_____ you,___ eight days a week is not e-nough to show I care.___

Ooh I need your love, babe, guess you know it's true.___
Love you ev-'ry day, girl,___ al-ways on my mind.___

Hope you need my love, babe,___ just like I need you.___ Hold me,___
One thing I can say, girl,___ love you all the time.___

love me.___ Hold me,___ love me.___ I ain't got noth-in' but

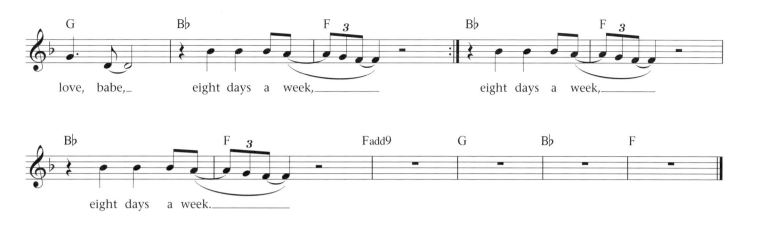

love, babe,___ eight days a week,_____ eight days a week,_____

eight days a week._____

Edelweiss

Words by
OSCAR HAMMERSTEIN II

Music by
RICHARD RODGERS

E - del - weiss, e - del - weiss, ev - 'ry morn - ing you greet

me. Small and white, clean and bright, you look

hap - py to meet me. Blos - som of snow, may you bloom and

grow, bloom and grow for - ev - er. E - del - weiss,

e - del - weiss, bless my home - land for - ev - er.

Enjoy Yourself
(It's Later Than You Think)

Words by
HERB MAGIDSON

Music by
CARL SIGMAN

1. You work and work for years and years, you're al - ways on the go. You
gon - na take that o - cean trip, no mat - ter come what may. You've

nev - er take a min - ute off, too bus - y mak - ing dough. Some day, you say, you'll
got your res - er - va - tions, but you just can't get a - way. Next year, for sure, you'll

have your fun when you're a mil - lion - aire. I - mag - ine all the
see the world, you'll real - ly get a - round. But how far can you

fun you'll have in your old rock - in' chair. En - joy your - self, it's
trav - el when you're six feet un - der ground? En - joy your - self, it's

lat - er than you think. En - joy your - self, while you're still in the pink. The

years go by as quick - ly as a wink. En - joy your - self, en - joy your - self, it's

1.
lat - er than you think. 2. You're

2.
lat - er than you think.

The Erie Canal

Traditional

Everybody Loves Somebody

Words by
IRVING TAYLOR

Music by
KEN LANE

Far Away Places

Words and Music by
ALEX KRAMER and JOAN WHITNEY

1. Far a - way pla - ces with strange sound - in' names, far a - way
2. call me a dream - er, well may - be I am. But I know that I'm

o - ver the sea. Those far a - way pla - ces with the
burn - in' to see those far a - way pla - ces with the

strange sound - in' names are call - in', call - in' me.
strange sound - in' names call - in', call - in' me.

Fine

Go - in' to Chi - na or may - be Si - am, I wan-na see for my -

self those far a - way pla - ces I've been read - in' a -

bout in a book that I took from a shelf. I start get - tin'

rest - less when - ev - er I hear the whis - tle of a train. I pray for the

D.C. al Fine

day I can get un - der - way and look for those cas - tles in Spain. (2.) They

Fields Of Gold

Music and Lyrics by
STING

walk in fields_ of gold._____

Man-y years have passed since those_
mem-ber me when the_

___ sum-mer days a-mong the fields_ of bar-ley.
___ west wind moves up-on the fields_ of bar-ley.

See the child-ren run as the
You can tell the sun in his

sun goes down a-mong___ the fields_ of gold.
jeal-ous sky when we walked in fields_ of gold,

1.
You'll re -

2.
when_ we

walked in fields_ of gold, when we walked in fields_ of gold._____

For He's A Jolly Good Fellow

Traditional

FIRST NOTE

Brightly

For he's a jol - ly good fel - low, for he's a jol - ly good fel - low, for

he's a jol - ly good fel - low, which no-bod-y can de - ny.___ Which

no - bo - dy can de - ny,___ which no - bo - dy can de - ny;___ for

he's a jol - ly good fel - low, which no - bo - dy can de - ny.___

Five Foot Two, Eyes Of Blue
(Has Anybody Seen My Gal?)

Words by JOE YOUNG
and SAM LEWIS

Music by
RAY HENDERSON

Folsom Prison Blues

Words and Music by
JOHN R. CASH

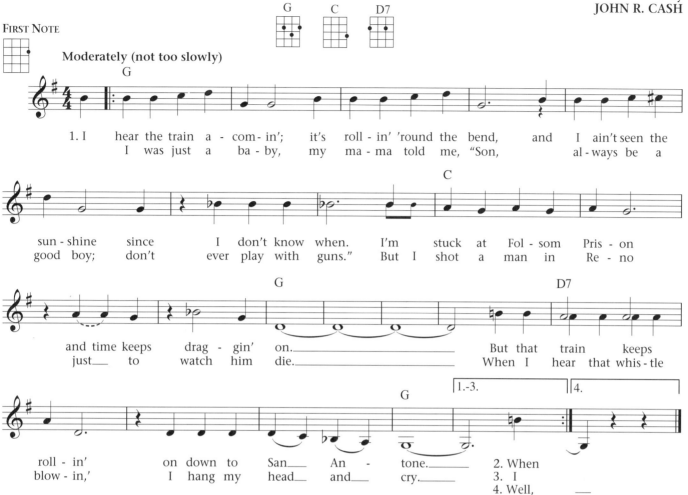

1. I hear the train a-com-in'; it's roll-in' 'round the bend, and I ain't seen the
   I was just a ba-by, my ma-ma told me, "Son, al-ways be a

sun-shine since I don't know when. I'm stuck at Fol-som Pris-on
good boy; don't ever play with guns." But I shot a man in Re-no

and time keeps drag-gin' on. But that train keeps
just to watch him die. When I hear that whis-tle

| 1.-3. | 4. |

roll-in' on down to San An-tone. 2. When
blow-in,' I hang my head and cry. 3. I
4. Well,

Additional Lyrics

3. I bet there's rich folks eatin' in a fancy dining car.
They're prob'ly drinkin' coffee and smokin' big cigars.
But I know I had it comin', I know I can't be free.
But those people keep a-movin', and that's what tortures me.

4. Well, if they freed me from this prison, if that railroad train was mine,
I bet I'd move on over a little farther down the line.
Far from Folsom Prison, that's where I want to stay,
and I'd let that lonesome whistle blow my blues away.

For Me And My Gal

Words by EDGAR LESLIE
and E. RAY GOETZ

Music by
GEORGE W. MEYER

Funiculì, Funiculà

Words by
EDWARD OXENFORD

Music by
LUIGI DENZA

From Me To You

Words and Music by JOHN LENNON
and PAUL McCARTNEY

F Dm C B♭7 C7 Cm F7 B♭ G7 C+ D♭+

FIRST NOTE

Moderately

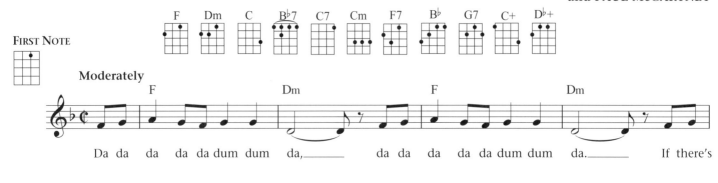

Da da da da da dum dum da,_____ da da da da da dum dum da._____ If there's

an - y - thing that you want,_____ if there's an - y - thing I can do,___
ev - 'ry - thing that you want,_____ like a heart__ that's oh so true,_

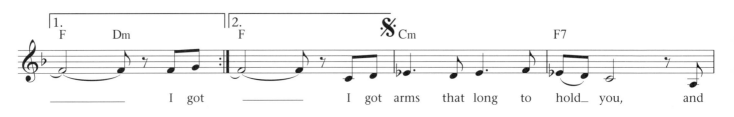

_____ just call on me__ and I'll send it a - long,__ with love__ from me__ to you.__

1.
2.

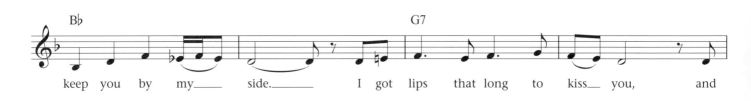

_____ I got _____ I got arms that long to hold__ you, and

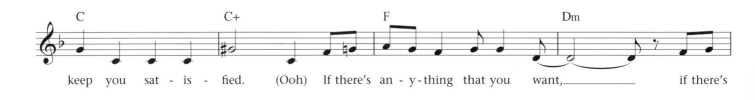

keep you by my__ side._____ I got lips that long to kiss__ you, and

keep you sat - is - fied. (Ooh) If there's an - y - thing that you want,_____ if there's

an - y - thing I can do,_____ just call on me____ and I'll

send it a-long,— with love— from me— to you.—

From— me to you.— Just call on me— and I'll

send it a-long,— with love— from me— to you.— I got

Coda

To you,— to you,— to you.

Georgia On My Mind

Words by
STUART GORRELL

Music by
HOAGY CARMICHAEL

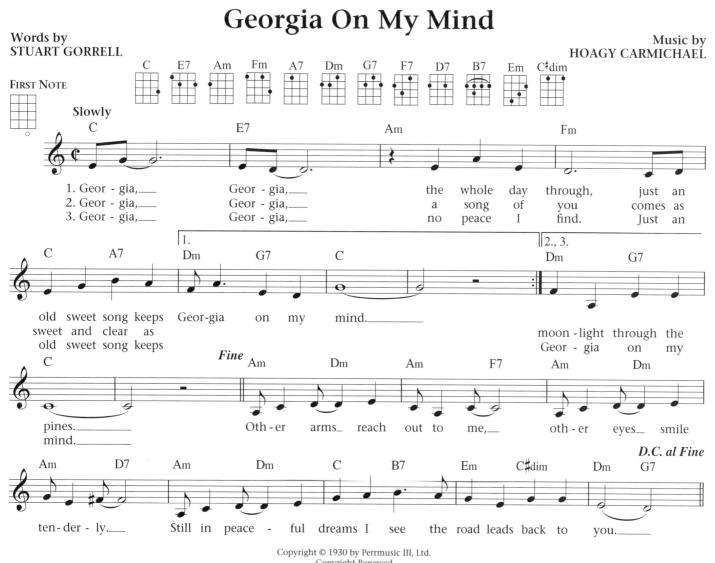

1. Geor - gia,— Geor - gia,— the whole day through, just an
2. Geor - gia,— Geor - gia,— a song of you comes as
3. Geor - gia,— Geor - gia,— no peace I find. Just an

old sweet song keeps Geor-gia on my mind.
sweet and clear as moon -light through the
old sweet song keeps Geor - gia on my

pines.———
mind.———
Oth - er arms— reach out to me,— oth - er eyes— smile

ten - der - ly.— Still in peace - ful dreams I see the road leads back to you.—

Getting To Know You

Lyricss by
OSCAR HAMMERSTEIN II

Music by
RICHARD RODGERS

Give My Regards To Broadway

Words and Music by
GEORGE M. COHAN

Give my re - gards to Broad - way, re - mem - ber me to Her - ald Square. Tell all the gang at For - ty - Se - cond Street that I will soon be there. Whis - per of how I'm yearn - ing to min - gle with the old - time throng. Give my re - gards to old Broad - way, and say that I'll be there, ere long.

Give Me That Old Time Religion

Traditional

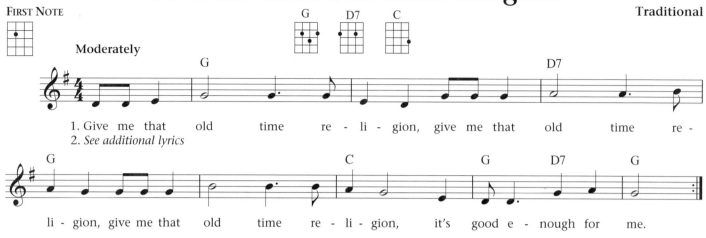

1. Give me that old time re - li - gion, give me that old time re -
2. *See additional lyrics*

li - gion, give me that old time re - li - gion, it's good e - nough for me.

Additional Lyrics

2. It was good for the Hebrew children,
   it was good for the Hebrew children,
   it was good for the Hebrew children,
   it's good enough for me.

3. It was good for our mothers,
   it was good for our mothers,
   it's good enough for me.

4. It will take us all to heaven,
   it will take us all to heaven,
   it will take us all to heaven,
   it's good enough for me.

The Glory Of Love

Words and Music by
BILLY HILL

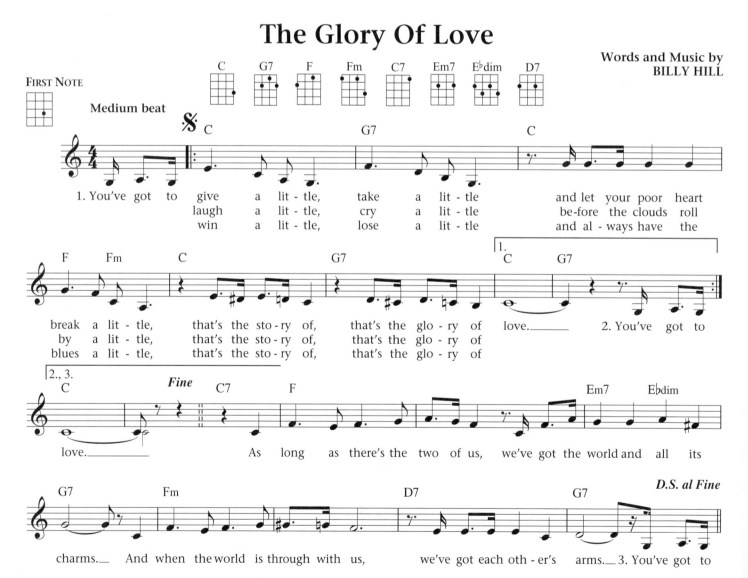

1. You've got to give a lit - tle, take a lit - tle and let your poor heart
   laugh a lit - tle, cry a lit - tle be-fore the clouds roll
   win a lit - tle, lose a lit - tle and al - ways have the

break a lit - tle, that's the sto - ry of, that's the glo - ry of love._____ 2. You've got to
by a lit - tle, that's the sto - ry of, that's the glo - ry of
blues a lit - tle, that's the sto - ry of, that's the glo - ry of

love._____ As long as there's the two of us, we've got the world and all its

charms.__ And when the world is through with us, we've got each oth - er's arms.__ 3. You've got to

Go Down, Moses

Traditional American Spiritual

1. When Is - rael was in E - gypt's land, let my peo - ple
2. No more shall they in bond - age toil, let my peo - ple

go. Op - pressed so hard they could not stand, let my peo - ple
go. Let them come out with E - gypt's spoil, let my peo - ple

go.
go. Go down, Mo - ses, 'way down in E - gypt's land.

Tell ole___ Pha - roah,___ let my peo - ple go.

Additional Lyrics

The Lord told Moses what to do, let my people go.
To lead the Hebrew children through, let my people go.
Chorus

O come along Moses, you'll not get lost, let my people go.
Stretch out your rod and come across, let my people go.
Chorus

As Israel stood by the waterside, let my people go.
At God's command it did divide, let my people go.
Chorus

When they reached the other shore, let my people go.
They sang a song of triumph o'er, let my people go.
Chorus

Pharaoh said he'd go across, let my people go.
But Pharaoh and his host were lost, let my people go.
Chorus

Jordan shall stand up like a wall, let my people go.
And the walls of Jericho shall fall, let my people go.
Chorus

Your foes shall not before you stand, let my people go.
And you'll possess fair Canaan's Land, let my people go.
Chorus

We need not always weep and mourn, let my people go.
And wear these slavery chains forlorn, let my people go.
Chorus

Good Day Sunshine

Words and Music by JOHN LENNON
and PAUL McCARTNEY

Good Night

Words and Music by JOHN LENNON and PAUL McCARTNEY

Now it's time to say good-night; good-night, sleep tight. Now the sun turns out his light, good-night, sleep tight. Dream sweet dreams for me. Dream sweet dreams for you.

Close your eyes and I'll close mine. Good-night, sleep tight.

Now the moon be-gins to shine.
Now the sun turns out his light.
Good-night, sleep tight.

Dream sweet dreams for me, dream sweet dreams for you.

Mm, mm, mm.

Coda

(Whispered) Good night good night ev'rybody. Ev'rybody, ev'rywhere, good night.

Goodnight, Irene

Words and Music by
HUDDIE LEDBETTER
and JOHN A. LOMAX

FIRST NOTE

Moderate waltz tempo

I - rene, good - night,_____ I - rene, good - night;_____ good -

night, I - rene, good - night, I - rene, I'll see you in my dreams._____

Fine

1. Last Sat - ur - day night I got mar - ried,_____ me and my wife set - tled
2. Some - times I live in the coun - try,_____ some - times I live in the
3. Stop ram - blin', stop your gam - blin',_____ stop stay - ing out late at_____

down._____ Now me and my wife_____ are part - ed,_____
town._____ Some - times I have a great no - tion_____
night._____ Go home to your wife and your fam - 'ly,_____

D.C. al Fine
last time

_____ I'm gon - na take an - oth - er walk_____ down - town._____
_____ to jump in - to the riv - er and drown._____
_____ sit down by the fire - side bright._____

Good Night Ladies

Words by E.P. CHRISTY

Traditional Music

Brightly

Good night la - dies,_ good night, la - dies!_ Good night,
Fare - well la - dies,_ fare - well, la - dies!_ Fare - well,
Sweet dreams, la - dies,_ sweet dreams, la - dies!_ Sweet dreams,

la - dies,_
la - dies,_ } we're going to leave you now. Mer - ri - ly we roll a - long,
la - dies,_

roll a - long, roll a - long. Mer - ri - ly we roll a - long, o'er the deep blue sea.

The Glow-Worm

English Words by
LILLA CAYLEY ROBINSON

German Words and Music by
PAUL LINCKE

Lightly

Shine, lit - tle glow-worm, glim - mer, (glim - mer,) shine, lit - tle glow-worm, glim - mer, (glim - mer.)

Lead us, lest too far we wan - der, love's sweet voice is call - ing yon - der!

Shine, lit - tle glow-worm, glim - mer, (glim - mer,) shine, lit - tle glow-worm, glim - mer, (glim - mer.)

Light the path, be - low, a - bove, and lead us on to love!___

A Groovy Kind Of Love

**Words and Music by TONI WINE
and CAROLE BAYER SAGER**

The 59th Street Bridge Song

(Feelin' Groovy)

Words and Music by
PAUL SIMON

Happy Together

Words and Music by
GARRY BONNER and
ALAN GORDON

Happy Trails

Words and Music by
DALE EVANS

FIRST NOTE

Some trails are hap-py ones,___ oth-ers are blue. It's the

way you ride the trail that counts;___ here's a hap-py one for you. Hap-py

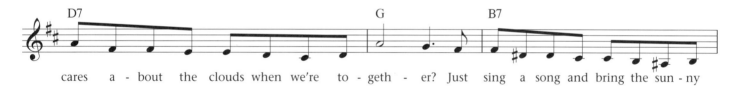

trails to you, un-til we meet a-gain. Hap-py

trails to you, keep smil-in' un-til then. Who

cares a-bout the clouds when we're to-geth-er? Just sing a song and bring the sun-ny

weath-er. Hap-py trails to you, 'til we meet a-gain.

A Hard Day's Night

Words and Music by JOHN LENNON and PAUL McCARTNEY

Hard Times Come Again No More

Words and Music by
STEPHEN FOSTER

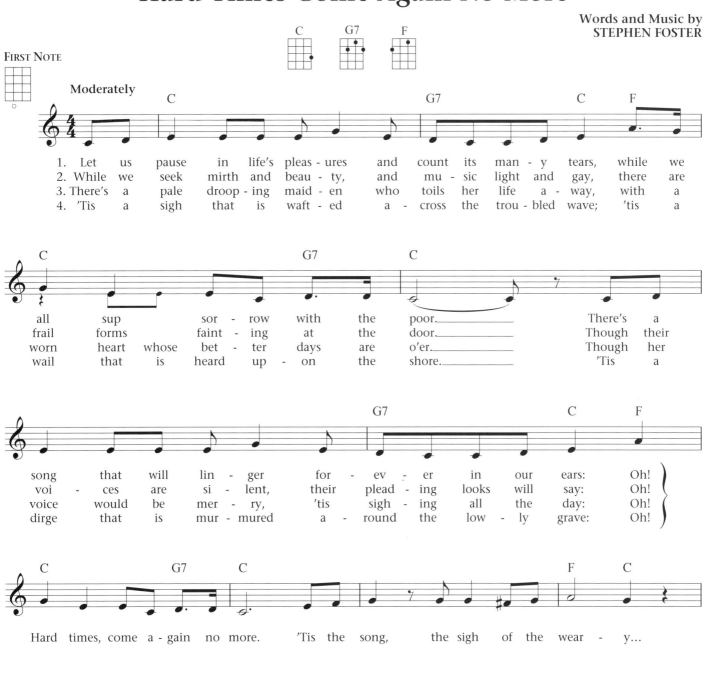

1. Let us pause in life's pleas-ures and count its man-y tears, while we
2. While we seek mirth and beau-ty, and mu-sic light and gay, there are
3. There's a pale droop-ing maid-en who toils her life a-way, with a
4. 'Tis a sigh that is waft-ed a-cross the trou-bled wave; 'tis a

all sup sor-row with the poor._____ There's a
frail forms faint-ing at the door._____ Though their
worn heart whose bet-ter days are o'er._____ Though her
wail that is heard up-on the shore._____ 'Tis a

song that will lin-ger for-ev-er in our ears: Oh!
voi-ces are si-lent, their plead-ing looks will say: Oh!
voice would be mer-ry, 'tis sigh-ing all the day: Oh!
dirge that is mur-mured a-round the low-ly grave: Oh!

Hard times, come a-gain no more. 'Tis the song, the sigh of the wear-y...

hard times, hard times come a-gain no more. Man-y days you have lin-gered a-

round my cab-in door; oh! hard times, come a-gain no more.

The Hawaiian Wedding Song

(Ke Kali Nei Au)

English Lyrics by
AL HOFFMAN and DICK MANNING

Hawaiian Lyrics and Music by
CHARLES E. KING

Hawaii Ponoi
(Hawaiian National Anthem)

Words and Music by
KING KALAKAUA
and HENRI BERGER

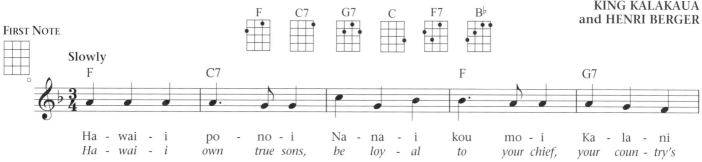

FIRST NOTE

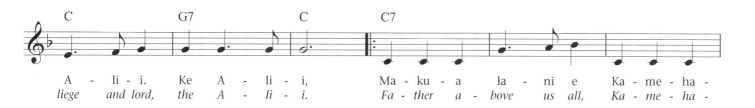

Slowly

Ha - wai - i po - no - i Na - na - i kou mo - i Ka - la - ni
Ha - wai - i own true sons, be loy - al to your chief, your coun - try's

A - li - i. Ke A - li - i, Ma - ku - a la - ni e Ka - me - ha -
liege and lord, the A - li - i. Fa - ther a - bove us all, Ka - me - ha -

me - ha e Na ka - ua e pa - le Me ka i - he.
me - ha e, who guard - ed in the war with his i - he.

Heart And Soul

Words by
FRANK LOESSER

Music by
HOAGY CARMICHAEL

Hello, Dolly!

Words and Music by
JERRY HERMAN

Help!

He's Got The Whole World In His Hands

Traditional Spiritual

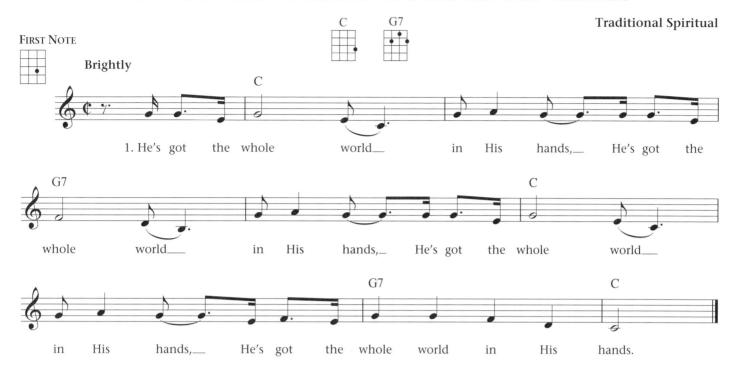

1. He's got the whole world__ in His hands,__ He's got the whole world__ in His hands,__ He's got the whole world__ in His hands,__ He's got the whole world in His hands.

Additional Lyrics

2. He's got the little bitty baby in His hands…
3. He's got you and me, sister, in His hands…
4. He's got you and me, brother, in His hands…
5. He's got a little ukulele in His hands…
6. He's got the whole world in His hands…

Hey, Good Lookin'

Words and Music by
HANK WILLIAMS

Hey Jude

Words and Music by
JOHN LENNON and
PAUL McCARTNEY

Home On The Range

Words by
DR. BREWSTER HIGLEY

Music by
DAN KELLY

Additional Lyrics

2. Oh, give me a land where the bright diamond sand
flows leisurely down the clear stream;
where the graceful white swan goes gliding along
like a maid in a heavenly dream.
Chorus

3. How often at night, when the heavens are bright
with the light from the glittering stars,
have I stood there amazed and asked as I gazed
if their glory exceeds that of ours.
Chorus

4. Where the air is so pure, and the zephyrs so free,
and the breezes so balmy and light,
that I would not exchange my home on the range
for all of the cities so bright.
Chorus

Hound Dog

Words and Music by
JERRY LEIBER and MIKE STOLLER

How Can I Keep From Singing?

Words and Music by
ROBERT LOWRY

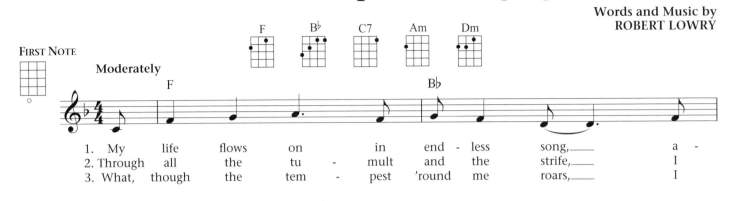

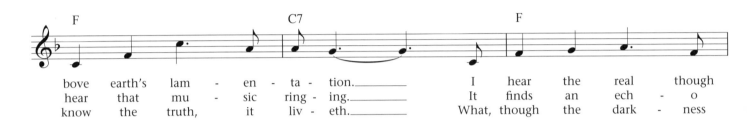

1. My life flows on in end - less song,____ a -
2. Through all the tu - mult and the strife,____ I
3. What, though the tem - pest 'round me roars,____ I

bove earth's lam - en - ta - tion.____ I hear the real though
hear that mu - sic ring - ing.____ It finds an ech - o
know the truth, it liv - eth.____ What, though the dark - ness

far - off hymn____ that hails a new cre - a - tion.____ } No
in my soul;____ how can I keep from sing - ing?____
gath - ers near,____ songs in the night it giv - eth.____

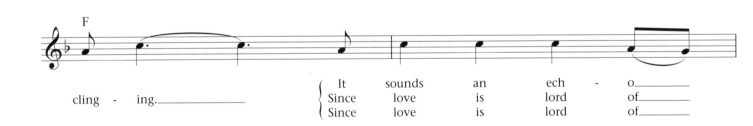

storm can shake my in - most calm,____ while to that rock I'm

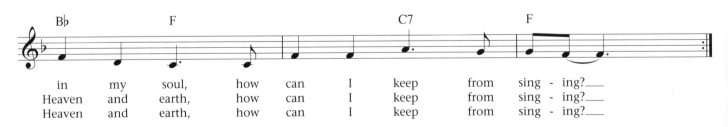

cling - ing.____ { It sounds an ech - o____
Since love is lord of____
Since love is lord of____

in my soul, how can I keep from sing - ing?___
Heaven and earth, how can I keep from sing - ing?___
Heaven and earth, how can I keep from sing - ing?___

How Can You Mend A Broken Heart

Words and Music by
BARRY GIBB and ROBIN GIBB

How Sweet It Is
(To Be Loved By You)

Words and Music by
EDWARD HOLLAND, LAMONT DOZIER,
and BRIAN HOLLAND

The Hukilau Song

Words and Music by
JACK OWENS

I Ain't Got Nobody
(And Nobody Cares For Me)

Words by
ROGER GRAHAM

Music by SPENCER WILLIAMS
and DAVE PEYTON

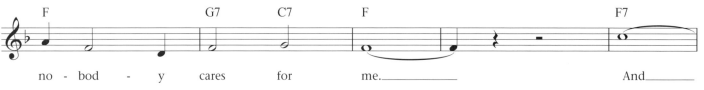

I_____ ain't got no - bod - y, and_____

no - bod - y cares for me._____ And_____

___ I'm sad and lone - ly, won't some - bod - y

come and take a chance with me?_____ I'll sing sweet

love songs, hon - ey, all the time, if you'll

come and be my sweet ba - by mine. I_____ ain't got no -

\- bod - y, and___ no - bod - y cares for me.

I Can't Give You Anything But Love

Words and Music by JIMMY McHUGH
and DOROTHY FIELDS

I Feel Fine

Words and Music by JOHN LENNON
and PAUL McCARTNEY

1. Ba - by's good to me, you know, she's hap - py as can be
2. Ba - by says she's mine, you know, she tells me all the time
3. ba - by buys her things, you know, he buys her dia - mond rings,

— you know, she said so. I'm in love with
— you know, she said so. I'm in love with
— you know, she said so. She's in love with

her and I feel fine.
her and I feel fine.
me and I feel fine.

I'm so glad that she's my lit - tle girl,

she's so glad she's tell - ing all the world that her

She's in love with me and I feel fine.

If I Had A Hammer
(The Hammer Song)

Words and Music by
LEE HAYS and PETE SEEGER

I Left My Heart In San Francisco

Words by
DOUGLASS CROSS

Music by
GEORGE CORY

I left my heart in San Fran-cis-co,_____ high on a hill, it calls to me. To be where lit-tle ca-ble cars_____ climb half-way to the stars!_____ The morn-ing fog_____ may chill the air; I don't care! My love waits there in San Fran-cis-co,_____ a-bove the blue_____ and wind-y sea. When I come home to you, San Fran-cis-co, your gold-en sun will shine for me!_____

I'll Be Seeing You

Words and Music by
IRVING KAHAL and SAMMY FAIN

1. I'll be see-ing you in all the old fa-mil-iar plac-es that this heart of
2. I'll be see-ing you in ev-'ry love-ly sum-mer's day, in ev-'ry-thing that's

mine em-brac-es all day through.___ In that small ca-fé, the park a-
light and gay, I'll

cross the way, the chil-dren's ca-rou-sel, the chest-nut trees, the wish-ing well.

al-ways think of you that way. I'll find you in the morn-ing sun, and when the night is

new, I'll be look-ing at the moon,___ but I'll be see-ing you!___

I'll Follow The Sun

Words and Music by JOHN LENNON
and PAUL McCARTNEY

One day__ you'll look__ to see I've gone.__ For to-mor-row may rain,__ so__

Some day__ you'll know__ I was the one,__ but to-mor-row may rain,__ so__

Instrumental   Yeah, to-mor-row may rain,__ so__

I'll fol-low the sun.

I'll fol-low the sun.

I'll fol-low the sun.

And now the time has come,__ and

so, my love,__ I must go.__ And though I lose a friend,__ in the end__ you will know:

Oh,__ one day__ you'll find__ that I have gone.__

D.C. (take 2nd ending)

But to-mor-row may rain,__ so__ I'll fol-low the sun.__

I'm A Believer

I'll Fly Away

Words and Music by
ALBERT E. BRUMLEY

Some glad morn-ing when this life is o'er___
When the shad-ows of this life have grown,_ } I'll fly a-way { to a home on
Just a few more wea-ry days and then___ } like a bird from
to a land where

God's ce-les-tial shore, }
pris-on bars has flown, } I'll fly a-way. I'll fly a-way, o glo-ry,
joys shall nev-er end, }

I'll fly a-way. When I die, hal-le-lu-jah by and by, I'll fly a-way.

In The Sweet By And By

Words by
SANFORD FILLMORE BENNETT

Music by
J. P. WEBSTER

1. There's a land that is fair-er than day, and by faith we can see it a-
sing on that beau-ti-ful shore, the me-lo-di-ous songs of the
boun-ti-ful Fa-ther a-bove, we will of-fer our trib-ute of

far, for the Fa-ther waits o-ver the way to pre-pare us a dwell-ing place
blessed, and our spir-its shall sor-row no more, not a sigh for the bless-ing of
praise for the glo-ri-ous gift of His love and the bless-ings that hal-low our

there. }
rest. } In the sweet by and by, we shall meet on that beau-ti-ful shore; in the
days. }

sweet by and by, we shall meet on that beau-ti-ful shore. 2. We shall
3. To our shore.

Imagine

Words and Music by
JOHN LENNON

I'm Always Chasing Rainbows

Words by
JOSEPH McCARTHY

Music by
HARRY CARROLL

I'm Beginning To See The Light

Words and Music by DON GEORGE,
JOHNNY HODGES, DUKE ELLINGTON,
and HARRY JAMES

FIRST NOTE

Medium Bounce

1. I nev-er cared much for moon-lit skies,_ I nev-er wink back at
2. nev-er went in for af-ter-glow__ or can-dle-light on the
3. nev-er made love by lan-tern shine._ I nev-er saw rain-bows

fi-re-flies,__ but now that the stars are in your eyes,_ I'm be-
mis-tle-toe,__ but now when you turn the lamp down low,__ I'm be-
in my wine;__ but now that your lips are burn-ing mine,__ I'm be-

1.
2., 3. *Fine*

gin-ning to see the light.__ I
gin-ning to see the light._
gin-ning to see the light._ ____ Used to ram-ble

through the park,_ shad-ow-box-ing in the dark._ Then you came and

D.S. al Fine

caused a spark__ that's a four-a-larm fi-re now.__ I

I'm Henry VIII, I Am

Words and Music by
FRED MURRAY and R.P. WESTON

Indiana

Words by
BALLARD MacDONALD

Music by
JAMES F. HANLEY

Back home a-gain in In-di-an-a, and it seems that I can see the gleam-ing can-dle-light still shin-ing bright through the syc-a-mores for me. The new-mown hay sends all its fra-grance from the fields I used to roam. When I dream a-bout the moon-light on the Wa-bash, then I long for my In-di-an-a home.

© 2010 Flea Market Music, Inc.

129

I Saw Her Standing There

Words and Music by JOHN LENNON
and PAUL McCARTNEY

In The Good Old Summertime

Words by
REN SHIELDS

Music by
GEORGE EVANS

I Saw The Light

Words and Music by
HANK WILLIAMS

It's Only A Paper Moon

**Words by BILLY ROSE
and E.Y. "Yip" HARBURG**

**Music by
HAROLD ARLEN**

1. Say, it's on-ly a pa-per moon___ sail-ing o-ver a
2. It's a Bar-num and Bai-ley world,___ just as phon-y as

card-board sea,___ but it would-n't be make-be-lieve___ if you___
it can be,___ but it would-n't be make-be-lieve___ if you___

— be-lieved in me.___ Yes, it's on-ly a can-vas sky___
— be-lieved in me.___

hang-ing o-ver a mus-lin tree,___ but it would-n't be make-be-lieve,___ if you___

— be-lieved in me.___ With-out your love, it's a hon-ky-tonk pa-rade. With-

out your love, it's a mel-o-dy played in a pen-ny ar-cade.

I've Been Working On The Railroad

American Folksong

I've Just Seen A Face

Words and Music by
JOHN LENNON
and PAUL McCARTNEY

I Want To Hold Your Hand

Words and Music by JOHN LENNON
and PAUL McCARTNEY

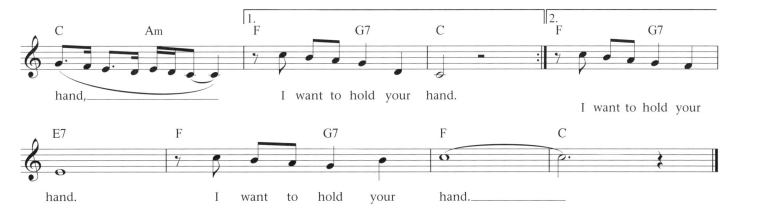

hand,___ I want to hold your hand.

I want to hold your

hand. I want to hold your hand.___

It's My Party

Words and Music by HERB WIENER,
WALLY GOLD, and JOHN GLUCK, JR.

A   C   D   F   B7   E7   A+   Dm

FIRST NOTE

Moderately

1. No - bod - y knows___ where my John - ny has gone,___ but
2. Play all my rec - ords, keep danc - ing all night,___ but
3. Ju - dy and John - ny just___ walked through the door,___

Ju - dy left___ the same time. Why was he hold-ing her hand,___ when
leave me a - lone___ for a while. 'Til John - ny's danc-ing with me,___ I've
like a queen___ with her king. Oh, what a birth-day sur - prise,___

he's sup - posed___ to be mine?___ It's my par - ty, and I'll
got no rea - son to smile.___
Ju - dy's wear - ing his ring.___

cry if I want___ to, cry if I want___ to, cry if I want___ to.

You would cry, too, if it hap -pened to you.

I Walk The Line

Words and Music by
JOHNNY CASH

1. I keep a close watch on this heart of mine.___ I keep my eyes wide
   ver - y, ver - y ea - sy to be true.___ I find my - self a -lone

o - pen all the time.___ I keep the ends out for the tie that binds.___
when each day is through.___ Yes, I'll ad - mit that I'm a fool for you.___

1.
___ Be - cause you're mine,___ I walk the line.___ 2. I find it
___ Be - cause you're mine,___ I walk the

2.
line.___

Additional Lyrics

3. As sure as night is dark and day is light,
   I keep you on my mind both day and night.
   And happiness I've known proves that it's right.
   Because you're mine, I walk the line.

4. You've got a way to keep me on your side.
   You give me cause for love that I can't hide.
   For you I know I'd even try to turn the tide.
   Because you're mine, I walk the line.

5. I keep a close watch on this heart of mine.
   I keep my eyes wide open all the time.
   I keep the ends out for the tie that binds.
   Because you're mine, I walk the line.

Ja-Da

Words and Music by
BOB CARLETON

Ja - Da___ Ja - Da,___ Ja - Da, Ja - Da jing, jing, jing. Ja - Da,___

Ja - Da,___ Ja - Da, Ja - Da, jing, jing, jing. That's a fun - ny lit - tle bit of

mel - o - dy.___ It's so sooth-ing and ap - peal - ing to me,___ it goes

Ja - Da,___ Ja - Da,___ Ja - Da, Ja - Da, jing, jing, jing.

Jackson

Words and Music by
BILLY EDD WHEELER
and JERRY LEIBER

Jambalaya
(On The Bayou)

Words and Music by
HANK WILLIAMS

Goodbye, Joe, me gotta go, me oh my oh. Me gotta go pole the
daux, Fontaineaux, the place is buzzin'. Kin folk come to see Y-

pirogue down the bayou. My Yvonne, the sweetest one, me oh my oh.
vonne by the dozen. Dress in style and go hog wild, me oh my oh.

Son-of-a-gun, we'll have big fun on the bayou. Jamba-
Son-of-a-gun, we'll have big fun on the bayou.

laya and a crawfish pie and fillet gumbo. 'Cause tonight I'm gonna see my macher a

mio. Pick guitar, fill fruit jar and be gayo. Son-of-a-

1. gun, we'll have big fun on the bayou. Thibo-

2. bayou.

Joshua Fought The Battle Of Jericho

African-American Spiritual

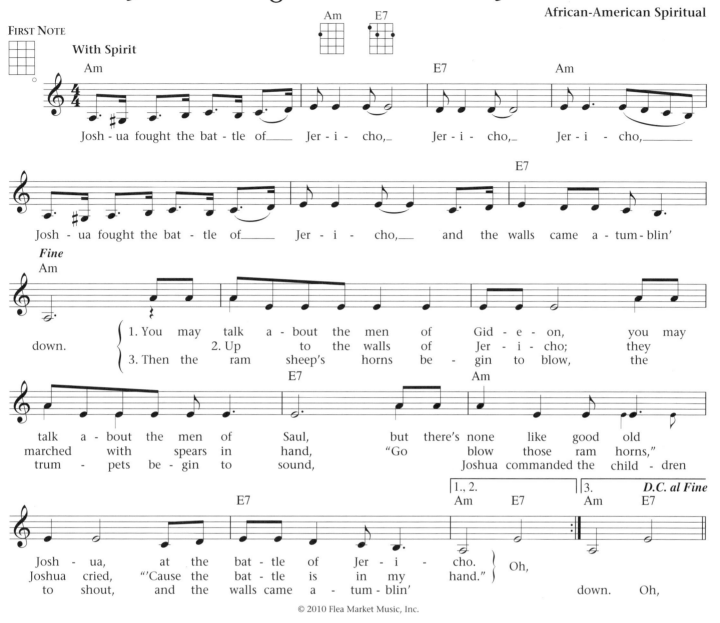

Joyful, Joyful, We Adore Thee

Words by
HENRY J. VAN DYKE

Music by
LUDWIG VAN BEETHOVEN

Keep On The Sunny Side

Words and Music by
A.P. CARTER

Bright and Sunny

1. There's a dark and a trou-bled side of life; there's a bright and a sun-ny side
   storm and its fu-ry broke to-day, crush-ing hopes that we cher-ish so
   greet with the song of hope each day, though the mo-ment be clou-dy or

too. Though we meet with the dark-ness and strife, the sun-ny side we al-so may view.
dear. Clouds and storm will in time pass a-way; the sun a-gain will shine bright and clear.
fair. Let us trust in our Sav-iour al-ways, who keep-eth ev-'ry-one in His care.

Keep on the sun-ny side, al-ways on the sun-ny side, keep on the sun-ny side of life.____ It will

help us ev-'ry day, it will bright-en all the way, if we keep on the sun-ny side of life. 2. The
3. Let us

Kumbaya

Traditional Spiritual

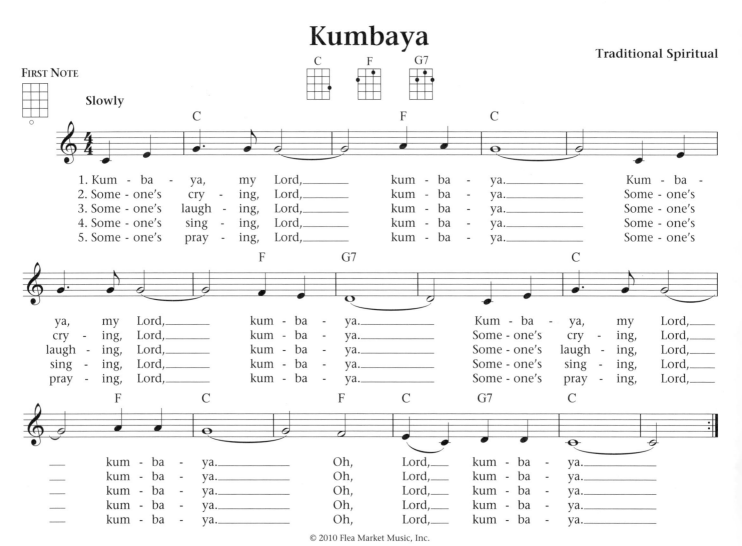

Slowly

1. Kum - ba - ya, my Lord,_____ kum - ba - ya._____ Kum - ba -
2. Some - one's cry - ing, Lord,_____ kum - ba - ya._____ Some - one's
3. Some - one's laugh - ing, Lord,_____ kum - ba - ya._____ Some - one's
4. Some - one's sing - ing, Lord,_____ kum - ba - ya._____ Some - one's
5. Some - one's pray - ing, Lord,_____ kum - ba - ya._____ Some - one's

ya, my Lord,_____ kum - ba - ya._____ Kum - ba - ya, my Lord,_____
cry - ing, Lord,_____ kum - ba - ya._____ Some - one's cry - ing, Lord,_____
laugh - ing, Lord,_____ kum - ba - ya._____ Some - one's laugh - ing, Lord,_____
sing - ing, Lord,_____ kum - ba - ya._____ Some - one's sing - ing, Lord,_____
pray - ing, Lord,_____ kum - ba - ya._____ Some - one's pray - ing, Lord,_____

—— kum - ba - ya._____ Oh, Lord,___ kum - ba - ya.
—— kum - ba - ya._____ Oh, Lord,___ kum - ba - ya.
—— kum - ba - ya._____ Oh, Lord,___ kum - ba - ya.
—— kum - ba - ya._____ Oh, Lord,___ kum - ba - ya.
—— kum - ba - ya._____ Oh, Lord,___ kum - ba - ya.

King Of The Road

Words and Music by
ROGER MILLER

Last Train To Clarksville

Words and Music by
BOBBY HART and TOMMY BOYCE

Let Me Call You Sweetheart

Words by
BETH SLATER WHITSON

Music by
LEO FRIEDMAN

Let me call you sweet-heart, I'm in love with you.

Let me hear you whis-per that you love me too.

Keep the love - light glow - ing in your eyes so true.

Let me call you sweet-heart, I'm in love with you.

Loch Lomond

Scottish Folksong

By___ yon bon - nie banks and by yon bon - nie braes, where the
O___ you'll take the high road and I'll take the low road, and___

sun shines bright on Loch Lo - mond, where me and my true love were
I'll be in Scot - land be - fore you. But me and my true love will

ev - er wont to be } on the bon-nie, bon-nie banks o' Loch Lo - mond.
nev - er meet a - gain }

Let It Be

**Words and Music by
JOHN LENNON and PAUL McCARTNEY**

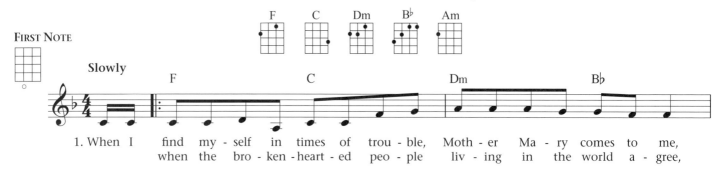

FIRST NOTE

1. When I find my-self in times of trou-ble, Moth-er Ma-ry comes to me,
when the bro-ken-heart-ed peo-ple liv-ing in the world a-gree,

speak-ing words of wis-dom, let it be._____ And
there will be an an-swer, let it be._____ For

in my hour of dark-ness she is stand-ing right in front of me.
though they may be part-ed, there is still a chance that they will see,

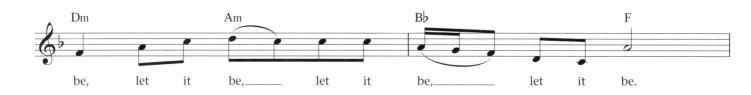

Speak-ing words of wis-dom, let it be.____ Let it
there will be an an-swer, let it be.____

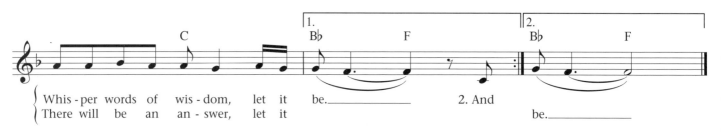

be, let it be,____ let it be,____ let it be.

1.
Whis-per words of wis-dom, let it be.____
There will be an an-swer, let it

2. And
2. And be.____

Let It Be Me
(Je T'appartiens)

English Words by
MANN CURTIS
French Words by
PIERRE DeLANOE

Music by
GILBERT BECAUD

Let's Get Together

Words and Music by
CHET POWERS

The Letter

Words and Music by
WAYNE CARSON THOMPSON

1.,3. Give me a tick-et for an air-plane, ain't got time to take the
2. I don't care how much mon-ey I got-ta spend, got to get back to my

fast-est train.
ba-by. Lone-ly days are gone, I'm a-go-in' home, my ba-by just wrote me a

1. let-ter.
2. let-ter. Well, she wrote me a let-ter, said she

could-n't live with-out me no more. Lis-ten, mis-ter, can't you see I

got to get back to my ba-by once more. An-y way.

Coda

let-ter. My ba-by just wrote me a let-ter. My

Let The Rest Of The World Go By

Words by
J. KEIRN BRENNAN

Music by
ERNEST R. BALL

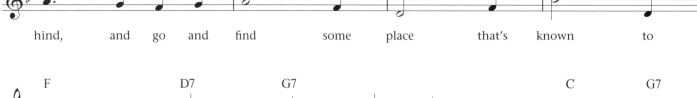

With some - one like you, a pal good and

true, I'd like to leave it all be -

hind, and go and find some place that's known to

God a - lone, just a spot to call our

own. We'll find per - fect peace, where joys nev - er cease, out

there be - neath a kind - ly sky._____ We'll build a

sweet lit - tle nest some - where in the West, and let the

rest of the world go by._____

Limehouse Blues

Words by
DOUGLAS FURBER

Music by
PHILIP BRAHAM

FIRST NOTE

Medium Swing

Oh, Lime - house kid, _____ oh, oh, oh, Lime - house kid _____

go - ing the way_____ that the rest of them did._____

Poor bro - ken blos - som and no - bod - y's child,_____

haunt - ing and taunt - ing, you're just kind o' wild._____ Oh, oh,

oh, lime - house blues,_____ I've the real lime - house blues,_____

can't seem to shake_____ off those sad Chi - na blues._____

Rings on your fin - gers and tears for your crown,_____

that is the sto - ry of old Chi - na - town._____

Long, Long Ago

Words and Music by
THOMAS BAYLY

Tell me the tales that to me were so dear, long, long a - go,
Do you re - mem - ber the path where we met, long, long a - go,
Tho' by your kind - ness my fond hopes were raised, long, long a - go,

long, long a - go. Sing me the songs I de - light - ed to hear,
long, long a - go? Ah yes, you told me you ne'er would for - get,
long, long a - go, you, by more el - o - quent lips, have been praised,

long, long a - go, long a - go. Now you are come, all my grief is re - moved;
long, long a - go, long a - go. Then to all oth - ers, my smile you pre - ferred;
long, long a - go, long a - go. But by long ab - sence your truth has been tried;

let me for - get that so long you have roved. Let me be - lieve that you
love, when you spoke, gave a charm to each word. Still my heart treas - ures the
still, to your ac - cents, I lis - ten with pride. Blest as I was when I

love as you loved, long, long a - go, long a - go.
prais - es I heard, long, long a - go, long a - go.
sat by your side, long, long a - go, long a - go.

© 2010 Flea Market Music, Inc.

152

Look For The Silver Lining

Words by
BUDDY DeSYLVA

Music by
JEROME KERN

Look for the sil - ver lin - ing when - e'er a cloud ap -

pears in the blue. Re - mem - ber some - where the sun is shin - ing

— and so the right thing to do is make it shine for you. A

heart full of joy and glad - ness will al - ways ban - ish

sad - ness and strife. So al - ways look for the sil - ver lin - ing

— and try to find the sun - ny side of life.

Love Me Do

Words and Music by
JOHN LENNON and
PAUL McCARTNEY

Love Me Tender

Words and Music by
ELVIS PRESLEY and
VERA MATSON

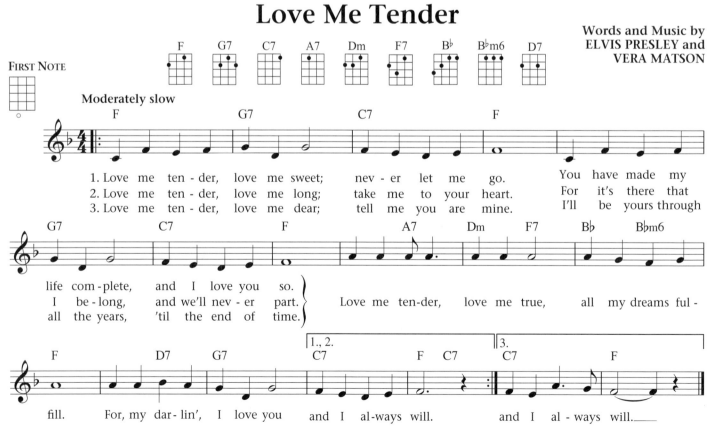

Love Potion Number 9

Words and Music by
JERRY LEIBER and MIKE STOLLER

Lovely Hula Hands

Words and Music by
R. ALEX ANDERSON

1. Love - ly hu - la hands grace - ful as the birds in mo - tion,____
2. Love - ly hu - la hands tell - ing of the rain in the val - ley____

____ glid - ing like the gulls o'er the o - cean,
____ and the swirl - ing wind on the pa - li, } love - ly hu - la

hands,__ kou - li - ma na - ni e. e. I can feel the soft ca -

ress - es of your love - ly hands,____ your love - ly hu - la hands.

Ev - 'ry lit - tle move ex - press - es so I'll un - der - stand all the ten - der mean - ing

of your hu - la hands, fin - ger-tips that say, "A - lo - ha."____

Say to me a - gain, "I love you!" Love - ly hu - la hands,_ kou - li - ma na - ni e.

Makin' Whoopee!

Words by
GUS KAHN

Music by
WALTER DONALDSON

Me And Bobby McGee

Words and Music by
KRIS KRISTOFFERSON
and FRED FOSTER

Feel-in' good was eas-y, Lord, when Bob-by sang the blues, and feel-in' good was
and, bud-dy, that was

good e-nough for me,_____ good e-nough for

good e-nough for me,_____

1. C
me and Bob-by Mc-Gee._____ From the

2. C
Gee._____

The Marine's Hymn

Words by
HENRY C. DAVIS

Melody based on a theme by
JACQUES OFFENBACH

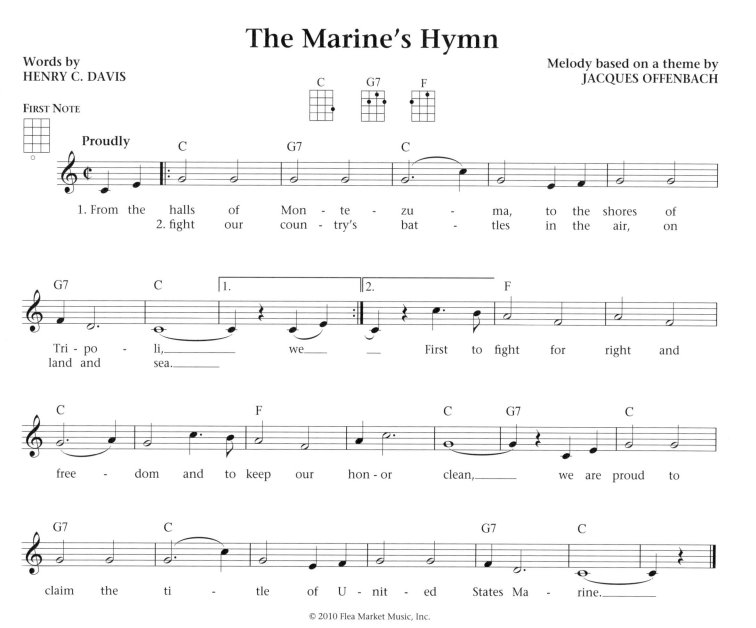

FIRST NOTE

Proudly

1. From the halls of Mon - te - zu - ma, to the shores of
2. fight our coun - try's bat - tles in the air, on

Tri - po - li,_____ we_____ First to fight for right and
land and sea._____

free - dom and to keep our hon - or clean,_____ we are proud to

claim the ti - tle of U - nit - ed States Ma - rine._____

Midnight Special

Railroad Song

FIRST NOTE

Bluesy

1. Well, you get up in the morn-ing, hear the work bell ring.
thing. Knife and fork are on the ta - ble, noth-in' in your pan.
2. *See additional lyrics*

You go a-march-in' to the ta - ble, you see the same damn
But if you say a word a - bout it, you're in____ trou - ble with the

Chorus

man. Let the mid - night spe - cial____ shine her light on me.

Fine   *D.C. al Fine*

Let the mid-night spe - cial____ shine her ev - er - lov - in' light on me.____

Additional Lyrics

2. Yonder comes Miss Rosie. How in the world did you know?
   By the way she wears her apron, and the clothes she wore.
   Umbrella on her shoulder, piece of paper in her hand.
   She come to tell the governor, "Turn loose of my man."
   Chorus

3. If you're ever in Houston, well you'd better walk right.
   You'd better not swagger, and you better not fight,
   or the sheriff will arrest you, he's gonna take you down.
   You can bet your bottom dollar, you're penitentiary bound.
   Chorus

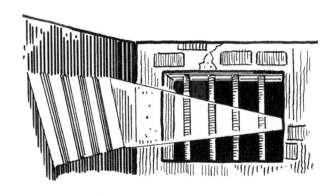

Michael, Row The Boat Ashore

Traditional Folksong

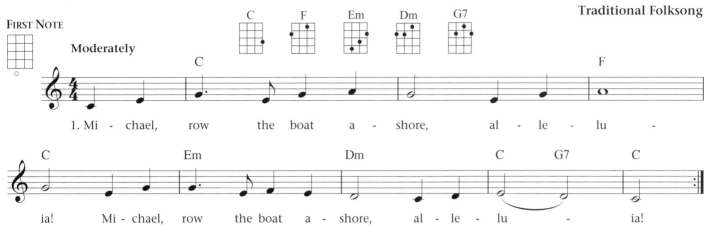

1. Mi - chael, row the boat a - shore, al - le - lu - ia! Mi - chael, row the boat a - shore, al - le - lu - ia!

Additional Lyrics

2. Michael's boat is a music boat, alleluia!
   Michael's boat is a music boat, alleluia!

3. Sister, help to trim the sail, alleluia!
   Sister, help to trim the sail, alleluia!

4. Jordan River is chilly and cold, alleluia!
   Chills the body, but not the soul, alleluia!

5. The river is deep and the river is wide, alleluia!
   Milk and honey on the other side, alleluia!

Mister Sandman

Words and Music by
PAT BALLARD

Boy: Mis - ter Sand - man bring me a dream,__ make her com - plex - ion like
Sand - man bring me a dream,__ make him the cut - est that

peach - es and cream.__ Give her two lips like ro - ses in clo - ver, then tell me
I've ev - er seen.__ Give him the word that I'm not a rov - er, then tell me

that my lone - some nights are o - ver. Sand - man, I'm so a - lone,__
that my lone - some nights are o - ver, Sand - man, I'm so a - lone,__

don't have no - bod - y to call my own.__ Please turn on__ your mag - ic beam,__

1.
__ Mis - ter Sand - man, bring me a dream.__ *Girl*: Mis - ter

Miss The Mississippi And You

Words and Music by
BILL HALLEY

Moon River

Words by
JOHNNY MERCER

Music by
HENRY MANCINI

My Favorite Things

Words by
OSCAR HAMMERSTEIN II

Music by
RICHARD RODGERS

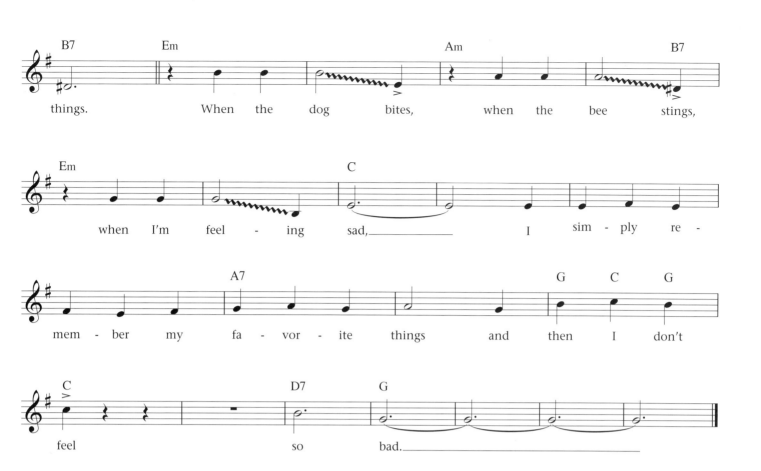

things. When the dog bites, when the bee stings,

when I'm feel - ing sad,_____ I sim - ply re -

mem - ber my fa - vor - ite things and then I don't

feel so bad._____

Moonlight Bay

Words by
EDWARD MADDEN

Music by
PERCY WENRICH

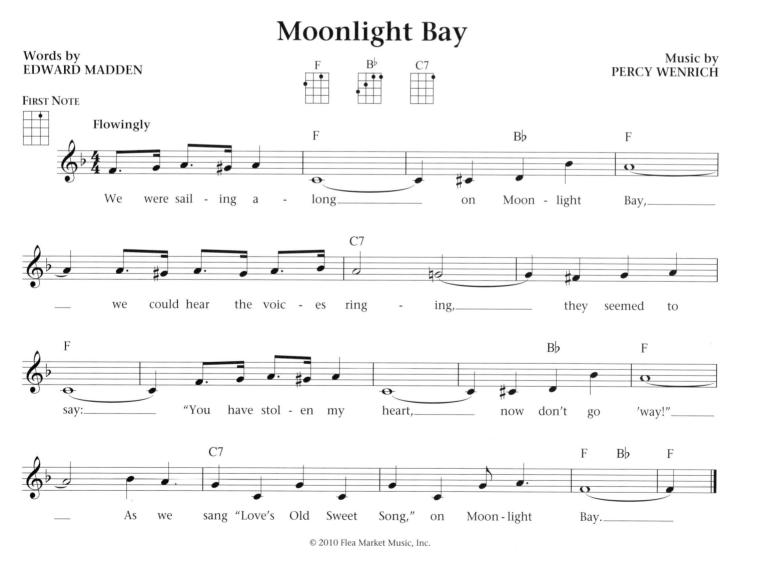

We were sail - ing a - long_____ on Moon - light Bay,_____

_____ we could hear the voic - es ring - ing,_____ they seemed to

say:_____ "You have stol - en my heart,_____ now don't go 'way!"

_____ As we sang "Love's Old Sweet Song," on Moon - light Bay._____

My Girl

Words and Music by
WILLIAM "SMOKEY" ROBINSON and
RONALD WHITE

My girl,_____ talk-ing 'bout my_ girl._____ I've got sun-shine on a

cloud - y day___ with my girl;_____ I've e - ven got the month of May with

my girl._____ Talk-ing 'bout,_ talk-ing 'bout,_ talk-ing 'bout,_ my girl._____ Woo!___

___ my girl.___ That's all___ I can talk a - bout, is my girl.

My Bonnie
(Lies Over The Ocean)

Traditional Scottish Song

My Bon - nie lies o - ver the o - cean,_____ my Bon - nie lies o - ver the

sea;_____ my Bon - nie lies o - ver the o - cean,_____ o, bring back my Bon - nie to

me._____ Bring back, bring back, o, bring back my Bon - nie to me, to

me. Bring back, bring back, o, bring back my Bon - nie to me._____

My Guy

Words and Music by
WILLIAM "SMOKEY" ROBINSON

My Blue Heaven

Words by
GEORGE WHITING

Music by
WALTER DONALDSON

My Love

Words and Music by
TONY HATCH

My Old Kentucky Home

Words and Music by
STEPHEN FOSTER

The Night Before

Words and Music by
JOHN LENNON and
PAUL McCARTNEY

Nobody Knows The Trouble I've Seen

African-American Spiritual

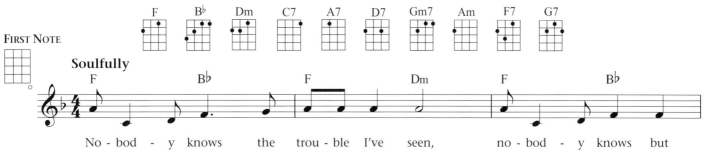

Soulfully

No - bod - y knows the trou - ble I've seen, no - bod - y knows but

Je - sus. No - bod - y knows the trou - ble I've seen,

glo - ry hal - le - lu - jah! 1. Some - times I'm up, some -
2.-4. *(See additional lyrics)*

times I'm down, oh, yes, Lord! Some -

times I'm al - most to the groun', _____ oh, yes, Lord!

Additional Lyrics

2. Now you may think that I don't know,
   oh, yes, Lord!
   But I've had troubles here below,
   oh, yes, Lord!

3. One day when I was walkin' along,
   oh, yes, Lord!
   the sky opened up and love came down,
   oh, yes, Lord!

4. I never shall forget that day,
   oh, yes, Lord!
   when Jesus washed my sins away,
   oh, yes, Lord!

Ob-La-Di, Ob-La-Da

Words and Music by
JOHN LENNON and
PAUL McCARTNEY

Oh, Babe, What Would You Say?

Words and Music by
E. S. SMITH

Oh, What A Beautiful Mornin'

Words by
OSCAR HAMMERSTEIN II

Music by
RICHARD RODGERS

Oh, Susanna

Words and Music by
STEPHEN FOSTER

FIRST NOTE

Moderately

1. I___ come from Al - a - bam - a with a ban - jo on my knee. I'm___ goin' to Lou' - si -
rained all night the day I left, the weath - er it was dry. The___ sun so hot I

3., 4. *See additional lyrics*

an - a, my Su - san - na for to see. 2. It___ cry. Oh, Su - san - na, oh
froze to death, Su - san - na don't you

don't you cry for me, for I come from Al - a - bam - a with a ban - jo on my knee.

Additional Lyrics

3. I had a dream the other night, when everything was still;
   I thought I saw Susanna a-coming down the hill.

4. The buckwheat cake was in her mouth, the tear was in her eye.
   Says I, "I'm coming from the South; Susanna, don't you cry!"

Old Folks At Home
(Swanee River)

Words and Music by
STEPHEN FOSTER

179

On A Slow Boat To China

Words and Music by
FRANK LOESSER

On Broadway

Words and Music by
BARRY MANN, CYNTHIA WEIL,
MIKE STOLLER, and JERRY LEIBER

FIRST NOTE

Moderately, with a beat

1. They say the ne - on lights are bright on Broad - way.
2. They say the girls are some - thin' else on Broad - way,
3. They say that I won't last too long on Broad - way.

They say there's al - ways ma - gic in the air.
but look - in' at them just gives me the blues.
I'll catch a Grey-hound bus for home they say.

But when you're walk - in' down that street and you ain't had e -
'Cause how ya gon - na make some time when all you got is
But they're dead wrong, I know they are, 'cause I can play this

1., 2.

nough to eat, the glit - ter rubs right off and you're no - where on
one thin dime and one thin dime won't e - ven shine your shoes. on
here gui - tar and I won't quit 'til

3.

Broad - way. I'm a star on Broad - way.
Broad - way.

© 1962, 1963 (Renewed 1990, 1991) SCREEN GEMS-EMI MUSIC INC.

Greetings From
NEW YORK BY NIGHT

On The Road Again

Words and Music by
WILLIE NELSON

1.,3. On the road a - gain._____ Just can't
road a - gain._____ Go - in'

wait to get on the road a - gain._____ The life I
pla - ces that I've_____ nev - er been._____ See - in'

love is mak - ing mu - sic with my friends, and
things that I may nev - er see a - gain and

I can't wait to get on the road__ a - gain._____ 2. On the
I can't wait to get on the road__ a -

gain._____ On the road a - gain,_____ like a

band of gyp - sies we go down the high - way._____ We're the

best of friends,_____ in - sist - ing that the world keep turn - ing

(Verse 1)
D.S. al Fine

our way,_____ and our way,_____ is on the

On The Sunny Side Of The Street

Words by
DOROTHY FIELDS

Music by
JIMMY McHUGH

FIRST NOTE

Moderately

1. Grab your coat, and get your hat, leave your wor - ry on the door - step;
   hear a pit - ter pat and that hap - py tune is your step;

just di - rect your feet to the sun - ny side of the street. 2. Can't you
life can be so sweet on the sun - ny side of the street. I used to

walk in the shade with those blues on par - ade, but I'm not a - fraid

this rov - er crossed o - ver. If I nev - er have a cent, I'll be rich as Rock - e -

fel - ler; gold dust at my feet on the sun - ny side of the street.

On Top Of Old Smoky

Kentucky Mountain Folksong

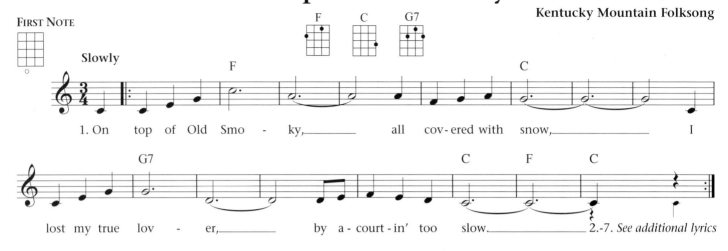

Slowly

1. On top of Old Smo - ky,_____ all cov-ered with snow,_____ I

lost my true lov - er,_____ by a - court - in' too slow._____ *2.-7. See additional lyrics*

Additional Lyrics

2. A-courtin's a pleasure, and parting is grief.
   But a false-hearted lover is worse than a thief.

3. A thief he will rob you and take all you have.
   But a false-hearted lover will send you to your grave.

4. They'll hug you and kiss you and tell you more lies
   than the cross-ties on the railroad, or the stars in the skies.

5. They'll tell you they love you, just to give your heart ease.
   But the minute your back's turned, they'll court whom they please.

6. So come all you young maidens and listen to me.
   Never place your affection on a green willow tree.

7. For the leaves they will wither and the roots they will die,
   and your true love will leave you, and you'll never know why.

On The Beach At Waikiki

Words by
G.H. STOVER

Music by
HENRY KAILIMAI

Brightly

1. "Ho - ni ka - u - a, wi - ki - wi - ki," sweet brown maid - en said to
2. "Ho - ni ka - u - a, wi - ki - wi - ki," she then said and smiled in
3. "Ho - ni ka - u - a, wi - ki - wi - ki," she re - peat - ed play - ful -
4. "Ho - ni ka - u - a, wi - ki - wi - ki," she was sure - ly teas - ing
5. "Ho - ni ka - u - a, wi - ki - wi - ki, you have learned it per - fect -

me_____ as she gave me lan - guage les - sons on the
glee,_____ but she would not trans - late for me on the
ly;_____ oh, those lips were so in - vit - ing on the
me,_____ so I caught that maid and kissed her on the
ly;_____ don't for - get what I have taught you," said the

beach at Wai - ki - ki.
beach at Wai - ki - ki.
beach at Wai - ki - ki.
beach at Wai - ki - ki.
maid at Wai - ki - ki._____

Peace Like A River

Spiritual

FIRST NOTE

Moderately

1. I've got peace like a riv-er, I've got peace like a
2. I've got love like an o-cean, I've got love like an
3. I've got joy like a foun-tain, I've got joy like a

riv-er, I've got peace like a riv-er in my soul._____ I've got
o-cean, I've got love like an o-cean in my soul._____ I've got
foun-tain, I've got joy like a foun-tain in my soul._____ I've got

peace like a riv-er, I've got peace like a riv-er, I've got
love like an o-cean, I've got love like an o-cean, I've got
joy like a foun-tain, I've got joy like a foun-tain, I've got

peace like a riv-er in_____ my soul!_____
love like an o-cean in_____ my soul!_____
joy like a foun-tain in_____ my soul!_____

Pearly Shells

Words and Music by
WEBLEY EDWARDS and LEON POBER

Pearl-y shells____ from the o - cean____ shin-ing in the sun,____ cov-er-ing the
Pu - pu____ a o e - wa____ i ka nu - ku____ e la-we

shore.____ When I see them____ my heart tells me that I love you more than
mai.____ A - he ai - na____ ma - i no____ a-la hu-la

all the lit - tle pearl - y shells. For ev - 'ry grain of sand up - on the beach, I've
pu-u-lo-a-he a-la he-le no ka-a- hu-pa - hau. I a - pau hu - na o - ne I ka ka-ha-

got a kiss for you; and I've got more left o - ver for each star that twin-kles in the blue. Pearl-y
kai ua ho - ni nau, ho'i ko - e la - wa na pa-ka-hi ho - ku 'i - mo i ka lani pu -

shells.____ More than all the lit - tle pearl - y shells.____
hau____ a-la hu-la pu-u-lo-a-he a-la he-le no ka-a-hu-pa - hau.____

186

Peggy Sue

Pennies From Heaven

Words by
JOHN BURKE

Music by
ARTHUR JOHNSTON

Ev - 'ry time it rains, it rains pen - nies from heav - en.

Don't you know each cloud con - tains pen - nies from heav - en?

You'll find your for - tune fall - ing all o - ver town.

Be sure that your um - brel - la is up - side down.

Trade them for a pack - age of sun - shine and flow - ers.

If you want the things you love, you must have show - ers.

So when you hear it thun - der, don't run un - der a tree, there'll be

pen - nies from heav - en for you and me.

Please Please Me

Words and Music by JOHN LENNON
and PAUL McCARTNEY

Princess Poo-Poo-Ly Has Plenty Pa-Pa-Ya
(And She Loves To Give It Away)

Words and Music by
HARRY OWENS

Proud Mary

Words and Music by
JOHN FOGERTY

Moderately (with a heavy beat)

Left a good job___ in the ci - ty,___ work-in' for The Man ev - 'ry
Cleaned a lot of plates in Mem - phis, pumped a lot of pain in

night and day,___ and I nev - er lost one min - ute of sleep - in'
New Or - leans,_ but I nev - er saw the good___ side of the ci - ty, un -

wor - ry - in' 'bout the way things might have been.___ Big wheel_ keep on___
til I hitched a ride on a riv - er - boat queen.___

turn - in'.___ Proud Mar - y keep on burn - in'! ___ Roll - in',___ roll -

- in',_ roll - in' on the riv - er.___ If you come down_ to the riv - er,

bet you gon - na find some peo - ple who live.___ You don't have to wor - ry___

'cause you have no mon - ey,___ peo - ple on the riv - er are hap - py to give.___

Coda

Roll- in',___ roll - in',___ roll-in' on the riv - er.___

Repeat ad lib and fade out

Que Sera, Sera
(Whatever Will Be, Will Be)

Words and Music by
JAY LIVINGSTON
and RAY EVANS

Raindrops Keep Fallin' On My Head

Words by
HAL DAVID

Music by
BURT BACHARACH

Rawhide

Words and Music by
DIMITRI TIOMKIN and
NED WASHINGTON

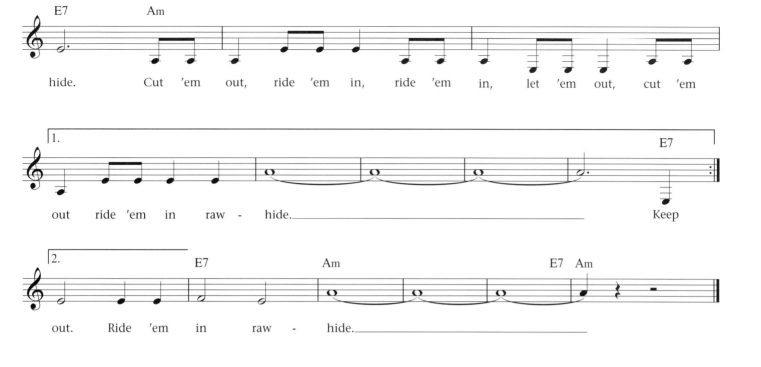

hide. Cut 'em out, ride 'em in, ride 'em in, let 'em out, cut 'em

1.

out ride 'em in raw - hide._____ Keep

2.

out. Ride 'em in raw - hide._____

Red River Valley

Traditional American Cowboy Song

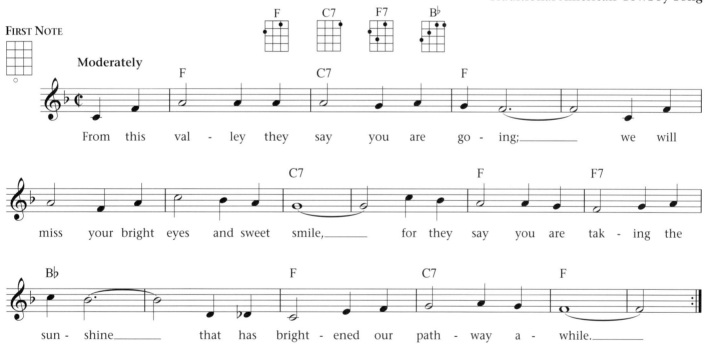

From this val - ley they say you are go - ing;_____ we will

miss your bright eyes and sweet smile,_____ for they say you are tak - ing the

sun - shine_____ that has bright - ened our path - way a - while._____

Additional Lyrics

2. Won't you think of this valley you're leaving?
Oh, how lonely, how sad it will be.
Oh, think of the fond heart you're breaking
and the grief you are causing me.

3. Come and sit by my side if you love me.
Do not hasten to bid me adieu,
but remember the Red River Valley
and the cowboy (cowgirl) that loves you so true.

Red Rubber Ball

Words and Music by PAUL SIMON
and BRUCE WOODLEY

Ring Of Fire

Words and Music by
MERLE KILGORE and
JUNE CARTER

Rock Around The Clock

Words and Music by MAX C. FREEDMAN
and JIMMY DeKNIGHT

Rocky Top

Words and Music by
BOUDLEAUX BRYANT and
FELICE BRYANT

Runaway

Words and Music by
DEL SHANNON and MAX CROOK

Rock-A My Soul

African-American Spiritual

Rock-a my soul__ in the bo-som of A - bra-ham; rock-a my soul__ in the

bo-som of A - bra-ham; rock-a my soul__ in the bo-som of A - bra-ham,

oh, rock-a my soul. His love is so high, you can't get o - ver it; so low, you

can't get un - der it; so wide, you can't get a - round__ it, you must go in at the door.

Runnin' Wild

Words by JOE GREY
and LEO WOOD

Music by
A. HARRINGTON GIBBS

Run-nin' wild,_____ lost con - trol,_____ run-nin' wild,_____

__ migh-ty bold,_____ feel-in' gay,_____ reck-less too,_____

__ care-free mind__ all the time__ nev-er blue._____ Al-ways goin',_____

__ don't know where;_____ al-ways showin', I don't care._____ Don't love no-

bod - y, it's not worth-while;__ all a - lone, run-nin' wild._____

Save The Last Dance For Me

Words and Music by DOC POMUS
and MORT SHUMAN

Second Hand Rose

Words by
GRANT CLARKE

Music by
JAMES F. HANLEY

Seems Like Old Times

Words and Music by
JOHN JACOB LOEB and
CARMEN LOMBARDO

Seems like old times, hav- ing you to walk with; seems like old
old times, din- ner dates and flow- ers, just like old

times, hav- ing you to talk with. And it's still a thrill just to
times, stay- ing up for hours.___ Mak- ing dreams come true, do- ing

1.
have my arms a- round you, still the thrill that it was the day I
things we used to

2.
found you. Seems like do, seems like old times,___ be- ing here with you.___

Sentimental Journey

Words and Music by
BUD GREEN, LES BROWN
and BEN HOMER

1. Gon - na take a sen - ti - men - tal jour - ney, gon - na set my
2. Got my bag, I got my res - er - va - tion; spent each dime I
3. Nev - er thought my heart could be so "yearn - y," why did I de -

heart at ease.___ Gon - na make a sen - ti - men - tal jour - ney
could af - ford.___ Like a child in wild an - ti - ci - pa - tion,
cide to roam?___ Got - ta take this sen - ti - men - tal jour - ney,

1., 3.

to re - new old mem - o - ries.___
long to hear that sen - ti - men - tal jour - ney home.__

2. *Fine*

"All___ a - board."___

Sev - en,___ that's the time we leave, at sev - en.___ I'll be wait - in' up for

D.C. al Fine

heav - en,___ count - in' ev - 'ry mile of rail - road track that takes me back.__

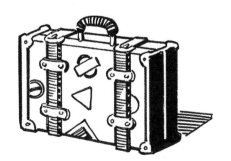

She Loves You

Words and Music by JOHN LENNON
and PAUL McCARTNEY

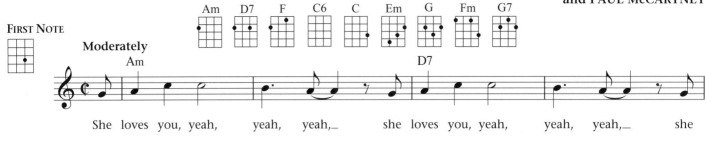

She loves you, yeah, yeah, yeah,_ she loves you, yeah, yeah, yeah,_ she

loves you, yeah, yeah, yeah, yeah._ You

think you've lost your love?_ Well, I saw her yes - ter - day._ It's

you she's think - ing of_ and she told me what to say._ She says, she

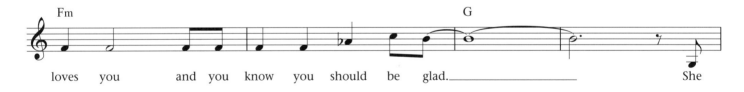

loves you and you know that can't be bad. Yes, she

loves you and you know you should be glad._ She

said you hurt her so,_ she al - most lost her mind._ But
know it's up to you,_ I think it's on - ly fair._

now she says she knows_ you're not the hurt - ing
Pride can hurt you too,_ a - pol - o - gize to

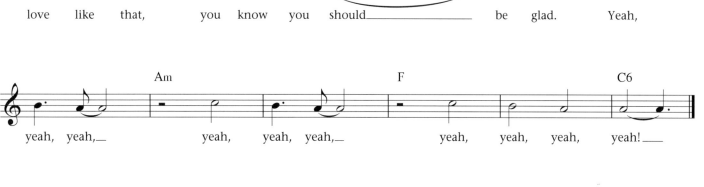

Shall We Gather At The River

Words and Music by
ROBERT LOWRY

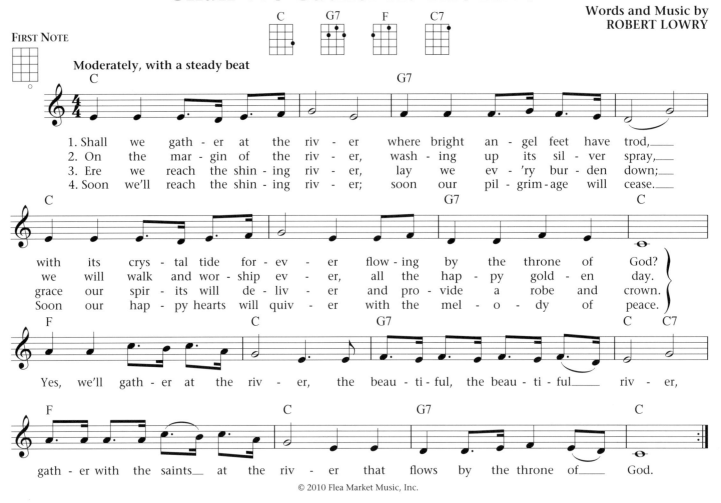

1. Shall we gath-er at the riv-er where bright an-gel feet have trod,___
2. On the mar-gin of the riv-er, wash-ing up its sil-ver spray,
3. Ere we reach the shin-ing riv-er, lay we ev-'ry bur-den down;___
4. Soon we'll reach the shin-ing riv-er; soon our pil-grim-age will cease.___

with its crys-tal tide for-ev-er flow-ing by the throne of God?
we will walk and wor-ship ev-er, all the hap-py gold-en day.
grace our spir-its will de-liv-er and pro-vide a robe and crown.
Soon our hap-py hearts will quiv-er with the mel-o-dy of peace.

Yes, we'll gath-er at the riv-er, the beau-ti-ful, the beau-ti-ful___ riv-er,

gath-er with the saints___ at the riv-er that flows by the throne of___ God.

Shenandoah

American Folksong

Slowly

1. Oh, Shen-an-doah,___ I long to hear you,___ a - way,___ you roll-ing

riv-er!___ Oh, Shen-an-doah,___ I long to hear you,___ a -

way,___ I'm bound a - way,___ 'cross the wide Mis-sou-ri!___

Additional Lyrics

2. Oh, Shenandoah, I love your daughter,
   away, you rolling river!
   For her, I'd cross the rolling water,
   away, I'm bound away, 'cross the wide Missouri.

3. Oh, Shenandoah, I'm bound to leave you,
   away, you rolling river!
   Oh, Shenandoah, I'll not deceive you,
   away, I'm bound away, 'cross the wide Missouri.

She'll Be Comin' 'Round The Mountain

Traditional

1. She'll be com-in' 'round the moun-tain when she comes,___ she'll be com-in' 'round the
2. She'll be driv-ing six white hors-es when she comes,___ she'll be driv-ing six white
3. Oh, we'll all go down to meet her when she comes,___ oh, we'll all go down to

moun-tain when she comes.___ She'll be com-in' 'round the moun-tain, she'll be
hors-es when she comes.___ She'll be driv-ing six white hors-es, she'll be
meet her when she comes.___ Oh, we'll all go down to meet her, oh, we'll

com-in' 'round the moun-tain, she'll be com-in' 'round the moun-tain when she comes.___
driv-ing six white hors-es, she'll be driv-ing six white hors-es when she comes.___
all go down to meet her, oh, we'll all go down to meet her when she comes.___

Shine On, Harvest Moon

Words by
JACK NORWORTH

Music by NORA BAYES
and JACK NORWORTH

Oh, shine on, shine on har-vest moon___ up in the sky. I ain't

had no lov-in' since Jan-u-ar-y, Feb-ru-ar-y, June or Ju-ly.___

Snow time ain't no time to stay___ out-doors and spoon, so

shine on, shine on har-vest moon, for me and my gal.

Sakura
(Cherry Blossoms)

Traditional Japanese Folksong

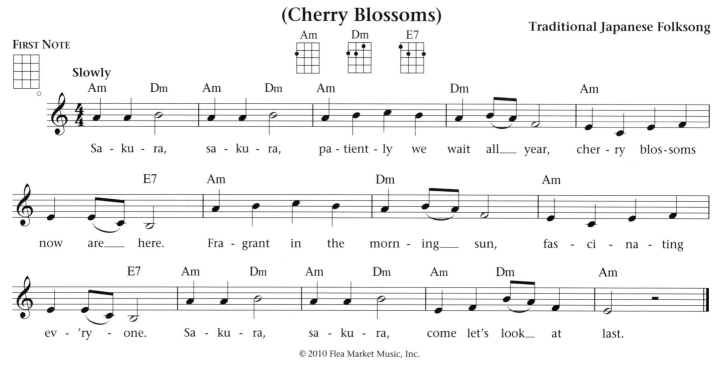

Sa - ku - ra, sa - ku - ra, pa - tient - ly we wait all___ year, cher - ry blos - soms now are___ here. Fra - grant in the morn - ing___ sun, fas - ci - na - ting ev - 'ry - one. Sa - ku - ra, sa - ku - ra, come let's look___ at last.

Side By Side

Words and Music by
HARRY WOODS

1. Oh! we ain't got a bar - rel of mon - ey,___
2. Don't know what's com - in' to - mor - row,___
(3.) all had their quar - rels and part - ed,___

may - be we're rag - ged and fun - ny;___ but we'll trav - el a - long___
may - be it's trou - ble and sor - row;___ but we'll trav - el the road,___
we'll be the same as we start - ed,___ just trav - 'lin a - long,___

sing - in' a song,___
shar - in' our load,___ side by side.
sing - in' a song,___

Through all kinds of wea - ther, what if the sky should fall? Just as long as we're to - geth - er, it does - n't mat - ter at all. 3. When they've

Sidewalks Of New York

Words and Music by
CHARLES B. LAWLOR and
JAMES W. BLAKE

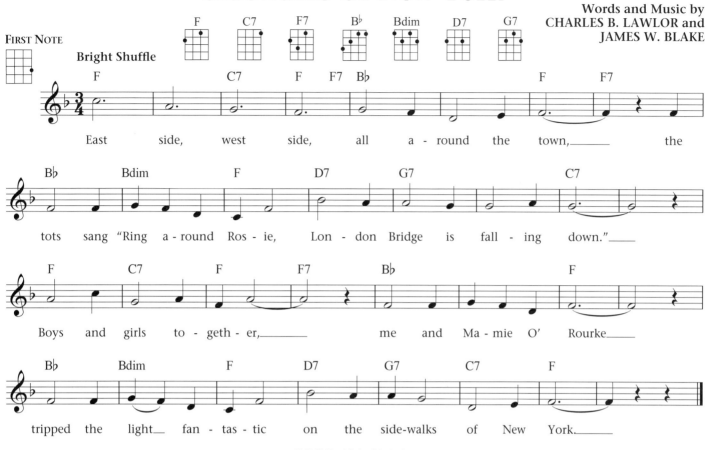

East side, west side, all a - round the town, ____ the tots sang "Ring a - round Ros - ie, Lon - don Bridge is fall - ing down." ____ Boys and girls to - geth - er, ____ me and Ma - mie O' Rourke ____ tripped the light ___ fan - tas - tic on the side - walks of New York. ____

Simple Gifts

Traditional Shaker Hymn

'Tis a gift to be sim - ple, 'tis a gift to be free, 'tis a gift to come down to where we ought to be. And when we find our - selves in the place just right, 'twill be in the val - ley of ___ love and de - light. When true sim - plic - i - ty is gained, to bow and to bend we ___ won't be a - shamed. To turn, turn, will be our de - light, 'til by turn - ing and turn - ing we ___ come a - round right.

Sing

Words and Music by
JOE RAPOSO

Sixteen Tons

Words and Music by
MERLE TRAVIS

The Sloop John B.

Traditional

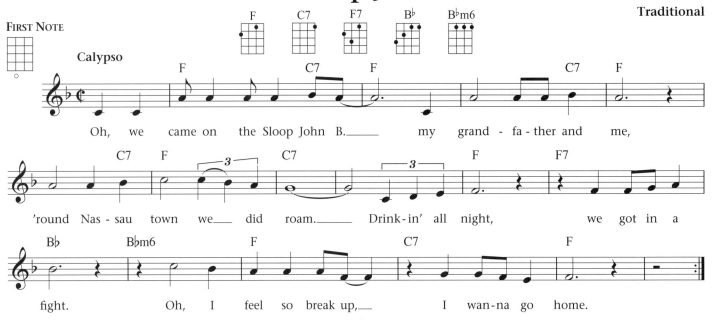

Oh, we came on the Sloop John B.___ my grand-fa-ther and me,
'round Nas-sau town we___ did roam.___ Drink-in' all night, we got in a
fight. Oh, I feel so break up,___ I wan-na go home.

Additional Lyrics

Chorus: (same chords as verse)
So hoist up the John B. sails,
see how the mainsail sets.
Send for the captain ashore, let me go home.
Let me go home, let me go home.
I feel so break up, I wanna go home.

2. The first mate, oh, he got drunk,
broke up the people's trunk,
Constable had to come and take him away.
Sheriff John Stone, please leave me alone.
I feel so break up, I wanna go home.
Chorus

3. The poor cook, oh, he got fits,
throw away all of the grits,
then he took and eat up all of my corn.
Let me go home, I want to go home.
This is the worst trip I've ever been on.
Chorus

Song Of The Islands

Words and Music by
CHAS. E. KING

1. Ha-wai-ian isles of beau-ty,___ where skies are blue and love is true;___ where balm-y
val-leys with their rain-bows,_ your moun-tains green, the a-zure sea.___ Your fra-grant
airs and gold-en moon-light___ ca-ress the wav-ing palms of Ho-no-lu-lu. 2. Your
flow'rs, en-chant-ing mu-sic___ u-nite and sing a-lo-ha oe to me.

Smiles

Words by
J. WILL CALLAHAN

Music by
LEE S. ROBERTS

There are smiles_____ that make us hap - py,_____ there are smiles_____ that make us blue,_____ there are smiles that steal a - way the tear - drops_____ as the sun - beams steal a - way the dew._____ There are smiles that have a ten - der mean - ing_____ that the eyes of love a - lone may see,_____ and the smiles that fill my life with sun - shine_____ are the smiles that you give to me._____

Some Folks

Words and Music by
STEPHEN FOSTER

FIRST NOTE

Moderately Fast

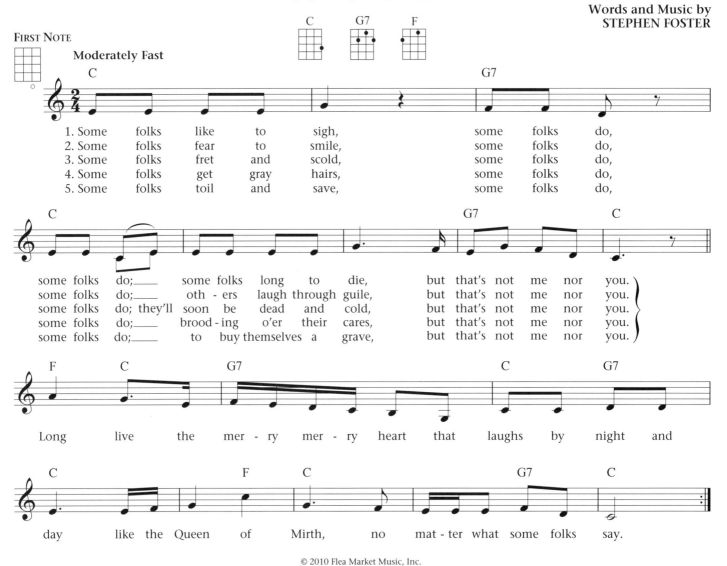

1. Some folks like to sigh,   some folks do,
2. Some folks fear to smile,   some folks do,
3. Some folks fret and scold,   some folks do,
4. Some folks get gray hairs,   some folks do,
5. Some folks toil and save,   some folks do,

some folks do;___ some folks long to die, but that's not me nor you.
some folks do;___ oth-ers laugh through guile, but that's not me nor you.
some folks do; they'll soon be dead and cold, but that's not me nor you.
some folks do;___ brood-ing o'er their cares, but that's not me nor you.
some folks do;___ to buy themselves a grave, but that's not me nor you.

Long live the mer-ry mer-ry heart that laughs by night and

day like the Queen of Mirth, no mat-ter what some folks say.

216

Some Of These Days

Words and Music by
SHELTON BROOKS

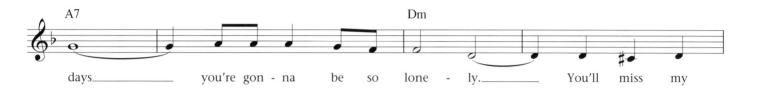

Some of these days_____ you'll miss_ me, hon - ey,_____ some of these

days_____ you're gon - na be so lone - ly._____ You'll miss my

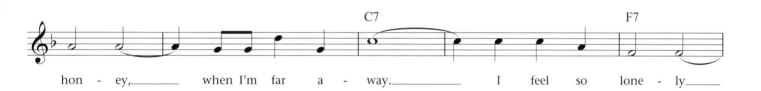

hug - ging,_____ you're gon - na miss my kiss - ing,_____ you're gon - na miss me

hon - ey,_____ when I'm far a - way._____ I feel so lone - ly_____

___ for you on - ly,_____ 'cause you know, hon - ey,_____ you've had your

way._____ And when you leave me,_____ you're gon - na grieve me,_____

_____ you'll miss_ your lit - tle ba - by,_____ yes, some_ of these days.

Song Sung Blue

Words and Music by
NEIL DIAMOND

Stand By Me

Words and Music by JERRY LEIBER,
MIKE STOLLER and BEN E. KING

Strangers In The Night

Words by
CHARLES SINGLETON
and EDDIE SNYDER

Music by
BERT KAEMPFERT

ev - er since that night,_____ we've been to - geth - er, lov - ers at first sight_____

_____ in love for - ev - er, it turned out so right____ for stran - gers in the night.____

The Star Spangled Banner

Words by
FRANCIS SCOTT KEY

Music by
JOHN STAFFORD SMITH

Oh,____ say, can you see, by the dawn's ear - ly light, what so
stripes and bright stars, through the per - il - ous fight, o'er the

proud - ly we hailed at the twi - light's last gleam - ing? Whose broad
ram - parts we watched were so gal - lant - ly stream - ing? And the

rock - et's red glare, the bombs burst - ing in air gave proof through the

night that our flag was still there. Oh, say does that____ star span - gled

ban - ner____ yet____ wave____ o'er the land____ of the free and the home of the brave.

Sunny Afternoon

Words and Music by
RAY DAVIES

The tax-man's tak-en all my dough, and left me in my
My girl-friend's run off with my car, and gone back to her

state-ly home,__ laz-ing on a sun-ny aft-er-noon. And I can't
ma and pa,__ tell-ing tales of drunk-en-ness and cruel-ty. Now I'm

sail my yacht, he's tak-en ev-'ry-thing I've got.__ All I've got's this
sit-ting here sip-ping at my ice-cold beer,__ laz-ing on a

sun-ny af-ter-noon.
sun-ny af-ter-noon. Save me, save me, save me from this
Help me, help me, help me sail a-

squeeze;__ I've got a big fat mom-ma tryin' to break__ me.
way;__ you give me two good rea-sons why I ought to stay.

And I love to live so plea-sant-ly, live this life of lux-u-ry,__
'Cause I love to live so plea-sant-ly, live this life of lux-u-ry,__

laz-ing on a sun-ny af-ter-noon,__ in sum-mer-time,__

__ in sum-mer-time,__ in sum-mer-time.__

Surfin' U.S.A.

Words and Music by
CHUCK BERRY

Sunrise, Sunset

Words by
SHELDON HARNICK

Music by
JERRY BOCK

Sun - rise,____ sun - set, sun - rise,____ sun - set, swift - ly____ fly the

years.____ One sea - son fol - low - ing an - oth - er, lad - en with

1. hap - pi - ness and tears.____

2. tears.____

Swanee

Words by
IRVING CAESAR

Music by
GEORGE GERSHWIN

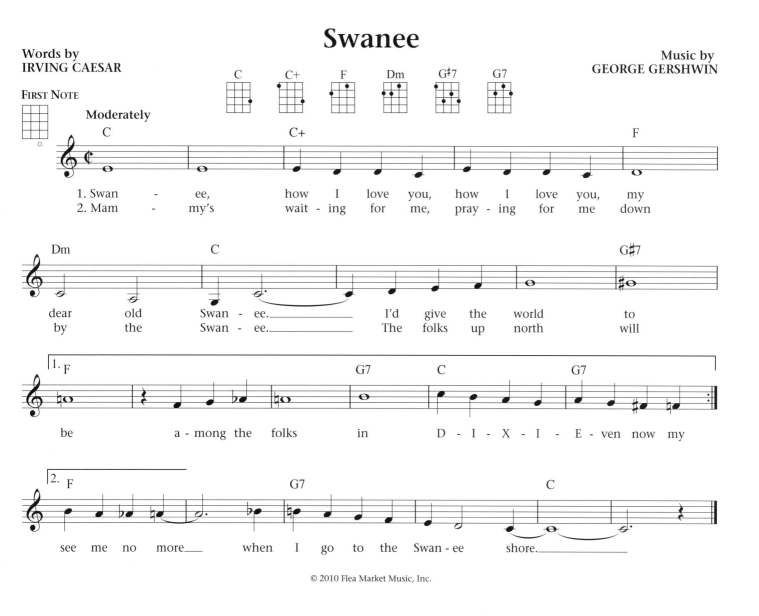

1. Swan - ee, how I love you, how I love you, my
2. Mam - my's wait - ing for me, pray - ing for me down

dear old Swan - ee.____ I'd give the world to
by the Swan - ee.____ The folks up north to will

1. be a - mong the folks in D - I - X - I - E - ven now my

2. see me no more____ when I go to the Swan - ee shore.____

Swing Low, Sweet Chariot

Traditional Spiritual

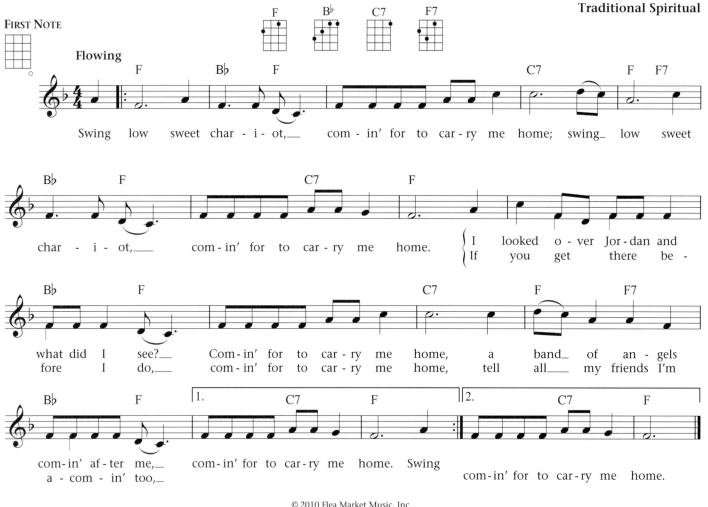

Swing low sweet char - i - ot,___ com - in' for to car - ry me home; swing_ low sweet
char - i - ot,___ com - in' for to car - ry me home.

I looked o - ver Jor - dan and
If you get there be -

what did I see?___ Com - in' for to car - ry me home, a band_ of an - gels
fore I do,___ com - in' for to car - ry me home, tell all___ my friends I'm

com - in' af - ter me,___ com - in' for to car - ry me home. Swing
a - com - in' too,___ com - in' for to car - ry me home.

Tell Me Why

American Folksong

1. Tell___ me why___ the stars do shine, tell___ me why___ the
2. Be - cause God made___ the stars to shine, be - cause God made___ the

i - vy twines. Tell___ me why___ the skies are blue,
i - vy twine. Be - cause God made___ the skies so blue,

and I will tell you why I___ love you.
be - cause God made you, that's why I love you.

226

Take Me Out To The Ballgame

Lyrics by
JACK NORWORTH

Music by
ALBERT VON TILZER

© 2010 Flea Market Music, Inc.

Taps

Traditional

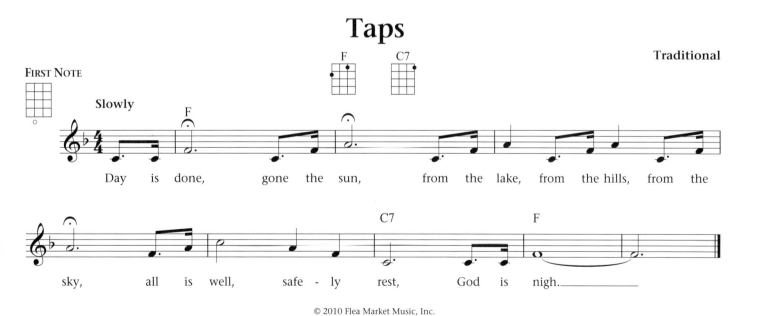

© 2010 Flea Market Music, Inc.

That Hawaiian Melody

Words and Music by
JIM BELOFF

1. From the land of sand and sea___ I brought home a mem - o - ry,
2. Gold - en sun and sil - ver rain,___ blue and em - 'rald is - land chain,

___ and it won't stop haunt - ing me,___
___ lin - ger like a sweet re - frain,___

that Ha - wai - ian mel - o - dy.
that Ha - wai - ian mel - o - dy. That warm and gen - tle

is - land greet - ing had me from the start.___ Ev - er since, it's

been re - peat - ing deep with - in my heart.

Palm trees sway a - gainst the moon,___ call - ing me to come back soon.

Such a charm - ing lit - tle tune, that Ha - wai - ian mel - o - dy.

That's Amoré
(That's Love)

Words by
JACK BROOKS

Music by
HARRY WARREN

When the moon hits your eye like a big piz-za pie, that's a-
When the stars make you drool just like pas-ta fa-zool, that's a-

mor - é._____ When the world seems to shine like you've
mor - é._____ When you dance down the street with a

To Coda ⊕

had too much wine, that's a - mor - é._____ Bells will ring, ting - a - ling - a -
cloud at your

ling, ting - a - ling - a - ling, and you'll sing "Vee - ta bel - la."_____ Hearts will

D.C. al Coda

play, tip - py - tip - py - tay, tip - py - tip - py - tay like a gay tar - an - tel - la._____

⊕ *Coda*

feet, you're in love._____ When you walk in a dream but you

know you're not dream - ing, sig - nor - é,_____ scuz - za me, but you

see, back in old Na - po - li, that's a - mor - é._____

That'll Be The Day

Words and Music by
JERRY ALLISON, NORMAN PETTY
and BUDDY HOLLY

There's A Kind Of Hush
(All Over The World)

Words and Music by LES REED
and GEOFF STEPHENS

These Boots Are Made For Walkin'

Words and Music by
LEE HAZLEWOOD

26 Miles
(Santa Catalina)

Words and Music by
GLEN LARSON and
BRUCE BELLAND

This Land Is Your Land

Words and Music by
WOODY GUTHRIE

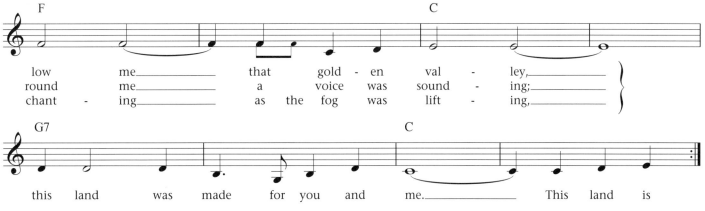

low me _____ that gold - en val - ley, _____
round me _____ a voice was sound - ing; _____
chant - ing _____ as the fog was lift - ing, _____

this land was made for you and me. _____ This land is

Additional Lyrics

4. In the squares of the cities, by the shadow of the steeples,
   in the relief office, I saw my people.
   And some were stumbling and some were wondering if
   this land was made for you and me.
   Chorus

5. As I went rambling that dusty highway,
   I saw a sign that said, "Private Property."
   But on the other side it didn't say nothing—
   that side was made for you and me.
   Chorus

6. Nobody living can ever stop me,
   as I go walking my freedom highway.
   Nobody living can make me turn back—
   this land was made for you and me.
   Chorus

This Little Light Of Mine

Traditional

1. This lit - tle light of mine, ___ I'm gon - na let it shine, ___
2. I've got the light of grace, ___ I'm gon - na let it shine, ___
3. We've got the light of love, ___ we're gon - na let it shine, ___

this lit - tle light of mine, ___ I'm gon - na let it shine, ___
I've got the light of grace, ___ I'm gon - na let it shine, ___
we've got the light of love, ___ we're gon - na let it shine, ___

this lit - tle light of mine, ___ I'm gon - na let it shine. ___ Let it shine, __
I've got the light of grace, ___ I'm gon - na let it shine. ___ Let it shine, __
we've got the light of love, ___ we're gon - na let it shine. ___ Let it shine, __

___ let it shine, ___ let it shine. _____
___ let it shine, ___ let it shine. _____
___ let it shine, ___ let it shine. _____

There Is A Tavern In The Town

Traditional Drinking Song

There is a tav - ern in the town, in the town, and there my
dieu, a - dieu, kind friend a - dieu, yes a - dieu I can no

true love sits him down, sits him down,_ and_ drinks his wine as mer - ry as can
long - er stay with you, stay with you,_ I'll_ hang my heart on a weep - ing wil - low

be and nev - er, nev - er thinks of me._
tree, and may the world go well with thee._ } Fare thee well, for I must leave thee, do not

let this part - ing grieve thee, for re - mem - ber that the best of friends must part, must part. A -

This Train

Traditional

1. This train is bound for glo - ry, this train._ This train is bound for glo - ry,
2.-3. *See additional lyrics*

this train._ This train is bound for glo - ry, don't ride noth - in' but the

right - eous and the ho - ly. This train is bound for glo - ry, this train._ this train._

Additional Lyrics

2. This train don't carry no gamblers, this train. (2x)
   This train don't carry no gamblers,
   no hypocrites, no midnight ramblers.
   This train is bound for glory, this train.

3. This train is built for speed now, this train. (2x)
   This train is built for speed now;
   fastest train you ever did see.
   This train is bound for glory, this train.

Three Little Birds

Words and Music by
BOB MARLEY

Those Were The Days

Words and Music by
GENE RASKIN

Freely

1. Once up-on a time there was a tav-ern
2. Then the bu-sy years went rush-ing by us. We
3. Just to-night I stood be-fore the tav-ern,
4. Through the door there came fa-mil-iar laugh-ter, I

where we used to raise a glass or two. Re-mem-ber how we laughed a-way the
lost our star-ry no-tions on the way. If by chance I'd see you in the
noth-ing seemed the way it used to be. In the glass I saw a strange re-
saw your face and heard you call my name. Oh, my friends we're old-er but no

hours,___ and dreamed of all the great things we would do.
tav-ern, we'd smile at one an-oth-er and we'd say:
flec-tion. Was that lone-ly fel-low real-ly me?
wis-er, for in our hearts the dreams are still the same.

Those were the

A Tempo

days, my friend,___ we thought they'd nev-er end.___ We'd sing and dance for-

ev-er and a day. We'd live the life we choose,___ we'd fight and

nev-er lose,___ for we were young and sure___ to have our way.

La la la la la la,___ la la la la la la,___ those were the

1., 2., 3.

days, oh yes, those were the days.

4.

days.___

The Times They Are A-Changin'

Words and Music by
BOB DYLAN

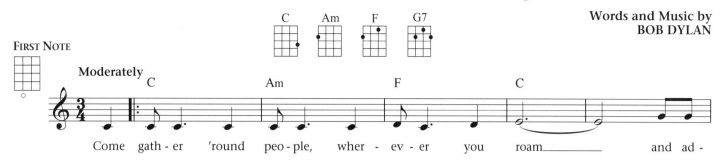

FIRST NOTE

Moderately

Come gath-er 'round peo-ple, wher-ev-er you roam_____ and ad -

mit that the wa-ters a - round you have grown, and ac - cept it that

soon you'll be drenched to the bone_____ if your time to you is worth

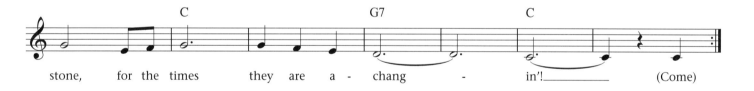

sav - in',_____ then you'd bet - ter start swim-min' or you'll sink like a

stone, for the times they are a - chang - in'!_____ (Come)

Additional Lyrics

2. Come writers and critics who prophesize with your pen,
and keep your eyes wide, the chance won't come again,
and don't speak too soon for the wheel's still in spin,
and there's no tellin' who that it's namin',
for the loser now will be later to win,
for the times they are a-changin'.

3. Come senators, congressmen, please heed the call
don't stand in the doorway, don't block up the hall.
For he that gets hurt will be he who has stalled.
There's a battle outside and it's ragin'.
It'll soon shake your windows and rattle your walls,
for the times they are a-changin'.

4. Come mothers and fathers throughout the land,
and don't criticize what you can't understand.
Your sons and your daughters are beyond your command,
your old road is rapidly agin'.
Please get out of the new one if you can't lend your hand,
for the times they are a-changin'.

5. The line it is drawn, the curse it is cast.
The slow one now will later be fast.
As the present now will later be past,
the order is rapidly fadin'.
And the first one now will later be last,
for the times they are a-changin'.

Tie Me Kangaroo Down Sport

Words and Music by
ROLF HARRIS

Moderately

Recitation over F chord

There's an old Australian stockman, dying. And he gets himself up on one elbow. And he turns to his mates, who are gathered 'round him and he says:

1. Watch me wal - la - bys feed, mate, watch me wal - la - bys feed.
2. Keep me cock - a - too cool, Curl, keep me cock - a - too cool.
3. Take me ko - a - la back, Jack, take me ko - a - la back.
4. Mind me plat - y - pus duck, Bill, mind me plat - y - pus duck.

They're a dan - ger - ous breed, mate, so watch me wal - la - bys
Don't go act - ing the fool, Curl, just keep me cock - a - too
He lives some-where out on the track, Mac, so take me ko - a - la
Don't let him go run - ning amok, Bill, mind me plat - y - pus

feed.
cool.
back.
duck.

Al - to - geth - er now! Tie me kan - ga - roo down sport,

tie me kan - ga - roo down. Tie me kan - ga - roo down, sport,

1.-5.

tie me kan - ga - roo down. Al - to - geth - er now! down.

6.

Additional Lyrics

5. Play your didgeridoo, Blue,
   play your didgeridoo.
   Keep playing 'til I shoot thro', Blue,
   Play your didgeridoo.

   Altogether now!

6. Tan me hide when I'm dead, Fred,
   tan me hide when I'm dead.
   So we tanned his hide when he died, Clyde,
   (Spoken) and that's it hanging on the shed.

   Altogether now!

Tiny Bubbles

Words and Music by
LEON POBER

Tonight You Belong To Me

Words by
BILLY ROSE

Music by
LEE DAVID

G   G7   Cmaj7   Cm6   D7   E9   A7

FIRST NOTE

Not too slow—play with a lilt

1. I know you be - long____ to some - bod - y
2. though we're a - part,____ you're part____ of my
3. know with the dawn____ that you____ will be

new;____ but to - night you be - long____ to me.
heart____ and to - night you be - long____ to me.
gone,____ but to - night you be - long____ to

To Coda

1.
Al -

2.
'Way down by the stream, how sweet it will

seem once more just to dream in the moon - light. My hon - ey, I

D.S. al Coda

Coda

me. Just to lit - tle old me!

Toot, Toot, Tootsie!
(Good-bye!)

Words and Music by
GUS KAHN, ERNIE ERDMAN,
DAN RUSSO and TED FIORITO

Try To Remember

Words by
TOM JONES

Music by
HARVEY SCHMIDT

Under The Boardwalk

Words and Music by
ARTIE RESNICK and
KENNY YOUNG

Turn! Turn! Turn!
(To Everything There Is A Season)

Words from the
BOOK OF ECCLESIASTES

Adaption and Music by
PETE SEEGER

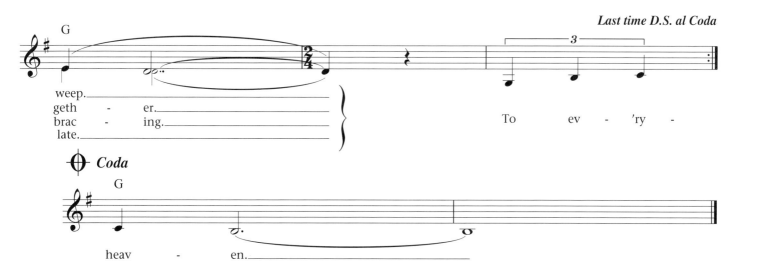

weep.
geth - er.
brac - ing.
late.

To ev - 'ry -

Coda

heav - en.

Unchained Melody

Words by
HY ZARET

Music by
ALEX NORTH

FIRST NOTE

Moderately slow

Oh, my love, my dar - ling, I've hun - gered for your touch a long, lone - ly

time. Time goes by so slow - ly and time can do so much, are you still

mine? I need your love, I need your love, God speed your love

to me! Lone - ly riv - ers flow to the sea, to the
Love - ly riv - ers sigh, "Wait for me, wait for

sea, to the o - pen arms of the sea.
me!" I'll be com - ing home, wait for me.

To You, Sweetheart, Aloha

Words and Music by
HARRY OWENS

To you, sweet-heart, a-lo-ha,____ a-lo-ha from the bot-tom of my heart.____ Keep the smile on your lips, brush the tear from your eye, one more a-lo-ha, then it's time for good-bye. To you, sweet-heart, a-lo-ha,____ in dreams I'll be with you, dear, to-night.____ And I'll pray for that day when we two will meet a-gain, un-til then sweet-heart, a-lo-ha.____

Ukuleles Are The Best

Words by ROBERT R. HALL, CHRISTOPHER R. REZEK,
GEOFFREY R. REZEK and JOSEPH P. REZEK

Music by CHRISTOPHER R. REZEK,
GEOFFREY R. REZEK, and JOSEPH P. REZEK

1. U-ku-le-les are the best, for-get a-bout the rest, we don't say in jest, u-ku-
2., 3., 4., etc. [Name] is the best, for-get a-bout the rest, we don't say in jest,

le-les are the best! [Name]_ is the best, be-cause we are all the best!
[Name] is the best!

Ukulele Lady

Words by
GUS KAHN

Music by
RICHARD A. WHITING

Up On The Roof

Words and Music by GERRY GOFFIN
and CAROLE KING

right smack dab in the mid-dle of town, I found a par-a-dise that's trou-ble

proof.___ And if this world starts get-ting you down, there's

room e-nough for two up on the roof.___

The Wabash Cannon Ball

Hobo Song

FIRST NOTE

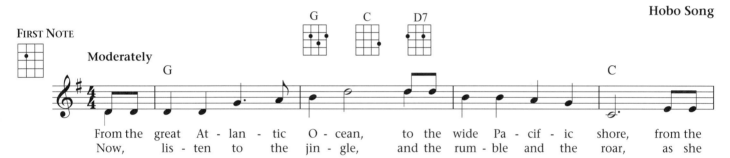

Moderately

From the great At-lan-tic O-cean, to the wide Pa-cif-ic shore, from the
Now, lis-ten to the jin-gle, and the rum-ble and the roar, as she

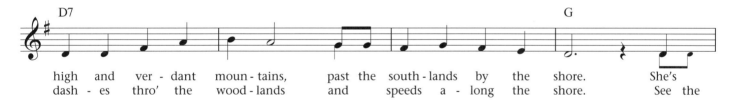

high and ver-dant moun-tains, past the south-lands by the shore. She's
dash-es thro' the wood-lands and speeds a-long the shore. See the

might-y tall and hand-some, and she's known quite well by all, she's a
might-y rush-ing en-gines, hear the mer-ry bell's clear call, as you

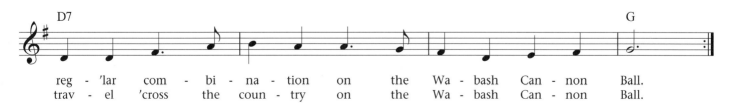

reg-'lar com-bi-na-tion on the Wa-bash Can-non Ball.
trav-el 'cross the coun-try on the Wa-bash Can-non Ball.

Wade In The Water

Traditional Spiritual

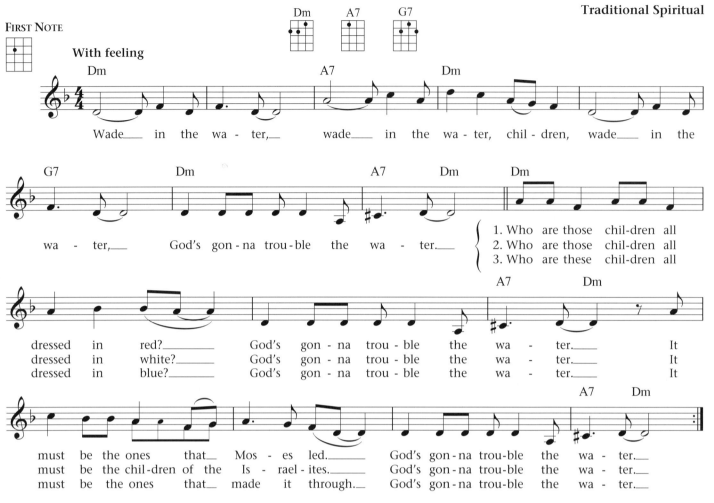

Wade— in the wa-ter,— wade— in the wa-ter, chil-dren, wade— in the

wa-ter,— God's gon-na trou-ble the wa-ter.—

1. Who are those chil-dren all
2. Who are those chil-dren all
3. Who are these chil-dren all

dressed in red?——— God's gon-na trou-ble the wa-ter.— It
dressed in white?——— God's gon-na trou-ble the wa-ter.— It
dressed in blue?——— God's gon-na trou-ble the wa-ter.— It

must be the ones that— Mos-es led.——— God's gon-na trou-ble the wa-ter.—
must be the chil-dren of the Is-rael-ites.——— God's gon-na trou-ble the wa-ter.—
must be the ones that— made it through.— God's gon-na trou-ble the wa-ter.—

The Water Is Wide

Traditional

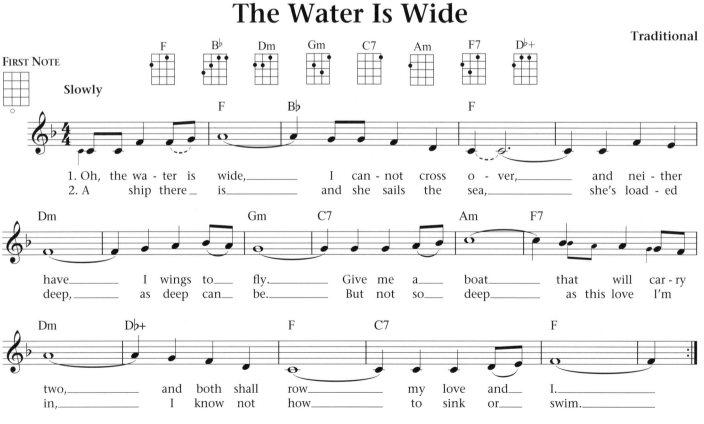

1. Oh, the wa-ter is wide,——— I can-not cross o-ver,——— and nei-ther
2. A ship there— is——— and she sails the sea,——— she's load-ed

have——— I wings to— fly.——— Give me a— boat——— that will car-ry
deep,——— as deep can be.——— But not so— deep——— as this love I'm

two,——— and both shall row——— my love and— I.———
in,——— I know not how——— to sink or— swim.———

Wake Up Little Susie

Words and Music by
BOUDLEAUX BRYANT
and FELICE BRYANT

Walkin' My Baby Back Home

Words and Music by
ROY TURK and FRED E. AHLERT

Additional Lyrics

She's afraid of the dark, so I had to park outside of her door 'til it's light.
She says if I try to kiss her she'll cry. I dry her tears all through the night.

Hand in hand to a barbeque stand, right from her doorway we roam.
Eats and then it's a pleasure again, walking my baby, talking my baby,
loving my baby, I don't mean maybe. Walking my baby back home

Walk Right In

Words and Music by
GUS CANNON and H. WOODS

Wayfaring Stranger

Traditional

Waltzing Matilda

Words by
A. B. PATERSON

Music by
MARIE COWAN

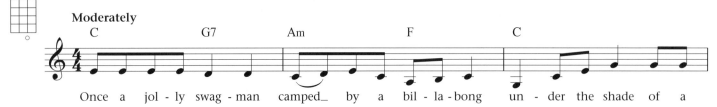

FIRST NOTE

Moderately

Once a jol-ly swag-man camped by a bil-la-bong un-der the shade of a

coo-li-bah tree, and he sang as he watched and wait-ed 'til his bil-ly boiled,

Chorus

"You'll come a-waltz-ing Ma-til-da with me!" Waltz-ing Ma-til-da,

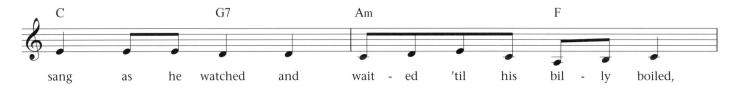

waltz-ing Ma-til-da, you'll come a-waltz-ing Ma-til-da with me. And he

sang as he watched and wait-ed 'til his bil-ly boiled,

"You'll come a-waltz-ing Ma-til-da with me!"

Additional Lyrics

2. Down came a jumbuck to drink at the billabong,
   up jumped the swagman and grabbed him with glee.
   And he sang as he stowed that jumbuck in his tucker bag,
   "You'll come a-waltzing Matilda with me!"
   Chorus

3. Up rode the squatter, mounted on his thoroughbred.
   Down came the troopers, one, two, three,
   "Where's that jolly jumbuck you've got in your tucker bag?"
   "You'll come a-waltzing Matilda with me!"
   Chorus

4. Up jumped the swagman, sprang into the billabong.
   "You'll never catch me alive," said he.
   And his ghost may be heard as you pass by that billabong,
   "You'll come a-waltzing Matilda with me!"
   Chorus

We Shall Overcome

Inspired by African American Gospel Singing,
members of the Food and Tobacco Workers Union, Charleston, SC
and the southern Civil Rights Movement

Musical and Lyrical Adaption by
ZILPHIA HORTON, FRANK HAMILTON,
GUY CARAWAN, and PETE SEEGER

FIRST NOTE

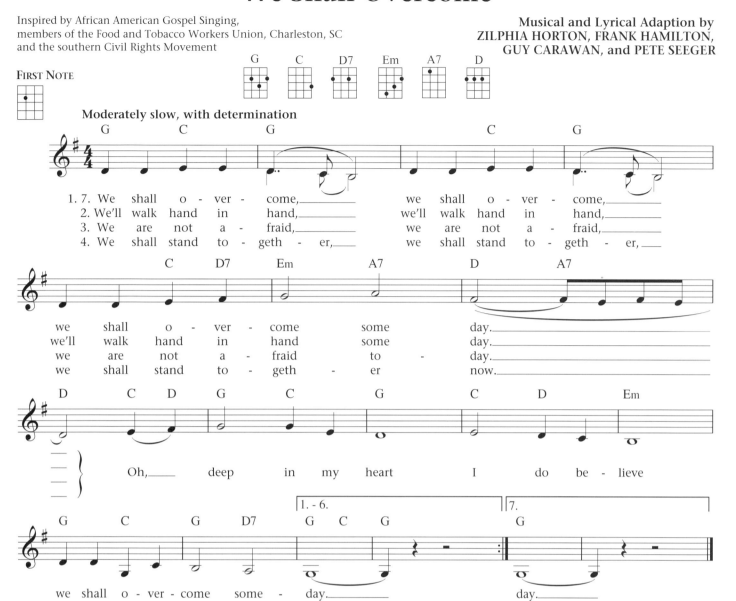

Moderately slow, with determination

1. 7. We shall o - ver - come,_____ we shall o - ver - come,_____
2. We'll walk hand in hand,_____ we'll walk hand in hand,_____
3. We are not a - fraid,_____ we are not a - fraid,_____
4. We shall stand to - geth - er,____ we shall stand to - geth - er, ____

we shall o - ver - come some day._____
we'll walk hand in hand some day._____
we are not a - fraid to - day._____
we shall stand to - geth - er now._____

Oh,____ deep in my heart I do be - lieve

we shall o - ver - come some - day._____

day._____

Additional Lyrics

5. The truth will make us free, the truth will make us free,
the truth will make us free someday, *etc.*

6. We shall live in peace, we shall live in peace,
we shall live in peace someday, *etc.*

What'll I Do?

Words and Music by
IRVING BERLIN

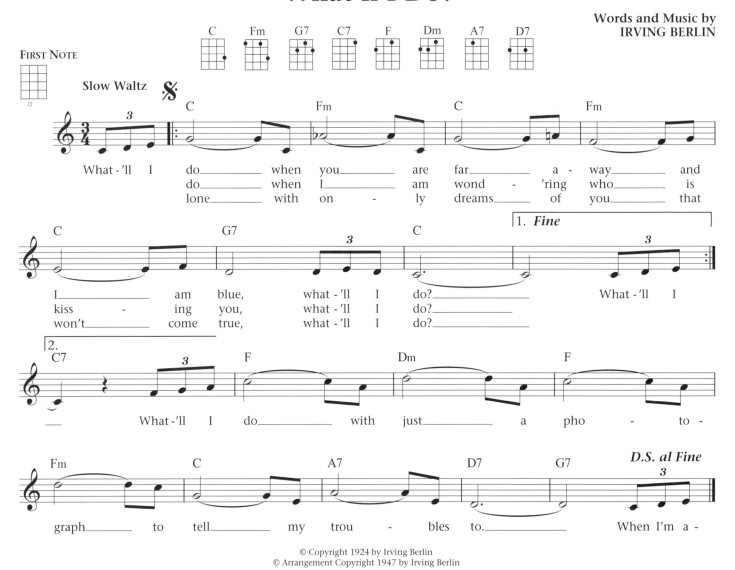

Slow Waltz

C   Fm   C   Fm

What-'ll I do_____ when you_____ are far_____ a-way_____ and
do_____ when I_____ am wond - 'ring who_____ is
lone_____ with on - ly dreams_____ of you_____ that

C   G7   C   1. *Fine*

I_____ am blue, what-'ll I do?_____ What-'ll I
kiss - ing you, what-'ll I do?_____
won't_____ come true, what-'ll I do?_____

2. C7   F   Dm   F

_____ What-'ll I do_____ with just_____ a pho - to -

Fm   C   A7   D7   G7   ***D.S. al Fine***

graph_____ to tell_____ my trou - bles to._____ When I'm a -

We'll Meet Again

Words and Music by ROSS PARKER
and HUGHIE CHARLES

What A Wonderful World

When I Fall In Love

Words by
EDWARD HEYMAN

Music by
VICTOR YOUNG

When I'm Sixty-Four

Words and Music by JOHN LENNON
and PAUL McCARTNEY

When I get old - er los-ing my hair_ man-y years from now,___

will you still be send-ing me a val-en-tine, __ birth-day greet-ings

bot-tle of wine?_ If I'd been out_ 'til quar-ter to three,_ would you lock the door?

__ Will you still need_ me, will you still feed_ me, when I'm six-ty-

four? Oo.___ You'll be old-er

too.___ Ah,___ and if you say the word,_ I could stay with

you. I could be hand-y mend-ing a fuse_
Send me a post-card drop me a line_

when your lights are gone.___ You can knit a sweat-er by the
stat-ing point of view.___ In-di-cate pre-cise-ly what you

When The Red, Red Robin
Comes Bob, Bob Bobbin' Along

Words and Music by
HARRY WOODS

When You're Smiling
(The Whole World Smiles With You)

Words and Music by
MARK FISHER, JOE GOODWIN
and LARRY SHAY

When You Wish Upon A Star

Words by
NED WASHINGTON

Music by
LEIGH HARLINE

When you wish up - on a star, makes no dif - f'rence who you are,
If your heart is in your dream, no re - quest is too ex - treme,

an - y - thing your heart de - sires will come to you.
when you wish up - on a star as dream - ers do. Fate is

kind, she brings to those who love the sweet ful - fill - ment of their se - cret

long - ing. Like a bolt out of the blue, fate steps in and

sees you through, when you wish up - on a star your dream comes true.____

When The Saints Go Marching In

Traditional

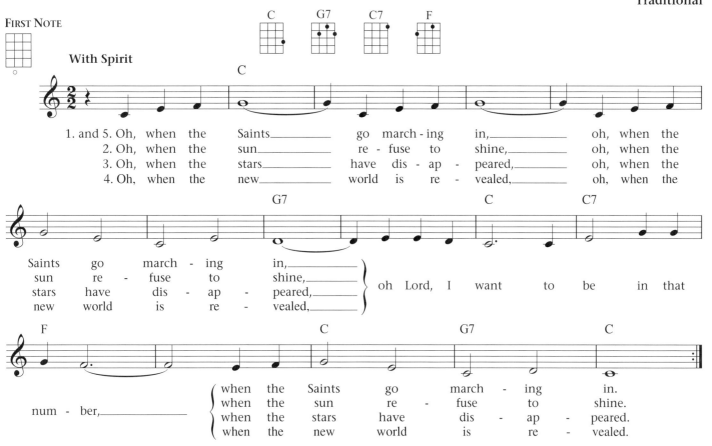

1. and 5. Oh, when the Saints go march-ing in, oh, when the
2. Oh, when the sun re-fuse to shine, oh, when the
3. Oh, when the stars have dis-ap-peared, oh, when the
4. Oh, when the new world is re-vealed, oh, when the

Saints go march-ing in, oh Lord, I want to be in that
sun re-fuse to shine,
stars have dis-ap-peared,
new world is re-vealed,

num-ber, when the Saints go march-ing in.
when the sun re-fuse to shine.
when the stars have dis-ap-peared.
when the new world is re-vealed.

© 2010 Flea Market Music, Inc.

Whispering

Words and Music by
RICHARD COBURN,
JOHN SCHONBERGER,
and VINCENT ROSE

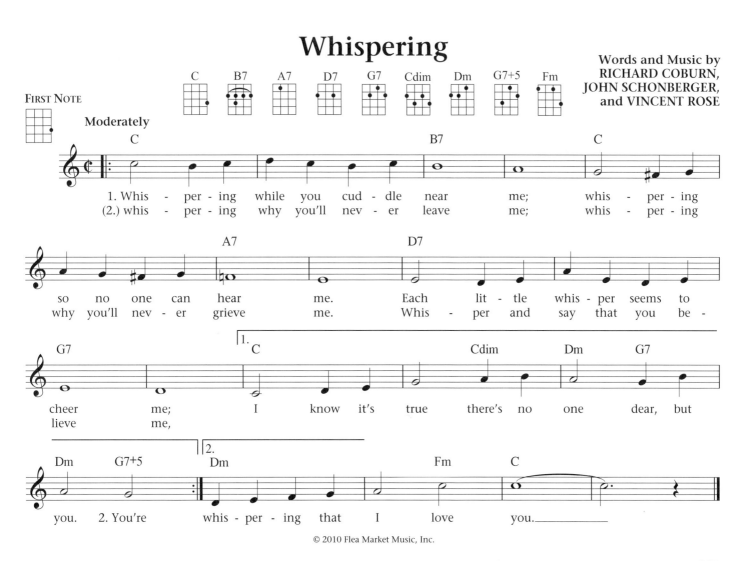

1. Whis-per-ing while you cud-dle near me; whis-per-ing
(2.) whis-per-ing why you'll nev-er leave me; whis-per-ing

so no one can hear me. Each lit-tle whis-per seems to
why you'll nev-er grieve me. Whis-per and say that you be-

cheer me; I know it's true there's no one dear, but
lieve me,

you. 2. You're whis-per-ing that I love you.

© 2010 Flea Market Music, Inc.

A White Sport Coat (And A Pink Carnation)

Words and Music by
MARTY ROBBINS

A white sport coat and a pink car-na-tion, I'm all dressed up for the dance. A white sport coat and a pink car-na-tion, I'm all a-lone in ro-mance. Once you told me long a-go to the prom with me you'd go. Now you've changed your mind, it seems, some-one else will hold my dreams. A white sport coat and a pink car-na-tion, I'm in a blue, blue mood.

Why Do Fools Fall In Love?

Words and Music by MORRIS LEVY
and FRANKIE LYMON

Why do birds sing so gay, and lov-ers a-wait the break of day? Why do they fall in love? Why does the rain fall from up a-bove? Why do fools fall in love? Why do they fall in love?

1. Love is a los-ing game, love can be a shame. I know of a fool, you see, for that fool is me! Tell me why, tell me why! Why do
2. Why does my heart skip a cra-zy beat? For I know it will reach de-feat! Tell me why, tell me why!

fools fall in love?

Wildwood Flower
(I'll Twine 'Mid the Ringlets)

Words by
MAUD IRVING

Music by
JOSEPH PHILBRICK WEBSTER

I'll twine 'mid the ring-lets of my ra-ven black hair, with the lil-lies so pale and the ro-ses so fair, and the myr-tle so bright with an em-er-ald hue, and the pale dais-y with eyes of bright blue.

Additional Lyrics

2. He told me he loved me and promised to love
through ill and misfortune all others above.
Another has won him, ah misery to tell;
he left me in silence with no word of farewell.

3. I'll dance and I'll sing and my laugh shall be gay.
I'll charm every heart in this crowd I survey.
And I'll long to see him regret the dark hour
when he'd gone and neglected his pale wildwood flower.

Will The Circle Be Unbroken

Words by
ADA R. HABERSHON

Music by
CHARLES H. GABRIEL

1. I was stand-ing by the win-dow on one cold and cloud-y
cir-cle be un-bro-ken, by and by, Lord, by and

day, and I saw the hearse come roll-ing for to
by? There's a bet-ter home a-wait-ing in the

car-ry my moth-er a-way. Oh, will the
sky, Lord, in the sky.

Additional Lyrics

2. Lord I told the undertaker,
"Undertaker, please drive slow,
for this body you are hauling,
Lord, I hate to see her go."
Chorus

3. I followed close behind her,
tried to hold up and be brave,
but I could not hide my sorrow
when they laid her in the grave.
Chorus

4. Went back home, Lord. My home was lonesome,
since my mother, she was gone.
All my brothers, sisters, crying,
what a home so sad and lone.
Chorus

World Without Love

Words and Music by JOHN LENNON
and PAUL McCARTNEY

With A Little Help From My Friends

Words and Music by
JOHN LENNON
and PAUL McCARTNEY

The World Is Waiting For The Sunrise

Words by
EUGENE LOCKHART

Music by
ERNEST SEITZ

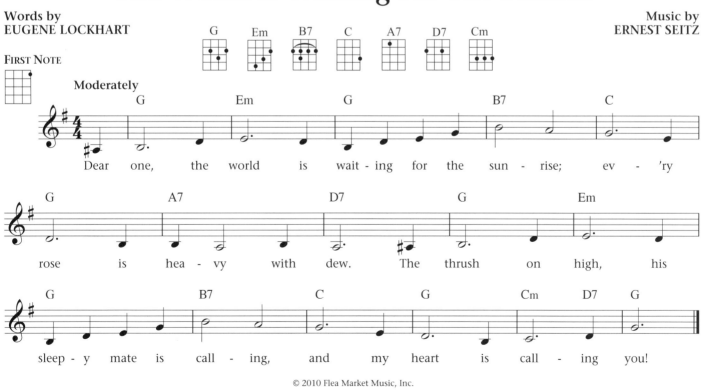

Wouldn't It Be Loverly

Words by
ALAN JAY LERNER

Music by
FREDERICK LOEWE

Gracefully

1. All I want is a room some-where, far a-way from the cold night air,
2. Lots of choc'-late for me to eat; lots of coal mak-in' lots of heat.
D.C. 3. Some-one's head rest-in' on my knee; warm and ten-der as he can be;

To Coda

with one e-nor-mous chair; oh, would-n't it be lov-er-ly?
Warm face, warm hands, warm feet, oh,
who takes good care of me, oh,

would-n't it be lov-er-ly? Oh, so lov-er-ly sit-tin' ab-so-bloom-in'-

D.C. al Coda

lute-ly still! I would nev-er budge 'til spring crept o-ver the win-dow-sill.

Coda

would-n't it be lov-er-ly? Lov-er-ly! Lov-er-ly! Lov-er-ly! Lov-er-ly!____

Wouldn't It Be Nice

Words and Music by
BRIAN WILSON, TONY ASHER
and MIKE LOVE

The Yellow Rose Of Texas

Traditional

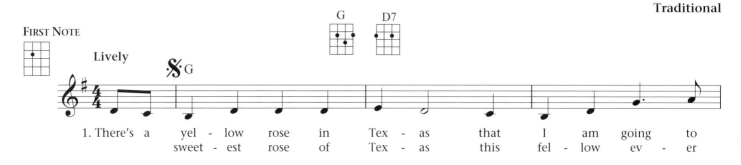

1. There's a yel - low rose in Tex - as that I am going to
sweet - est rose of Tex - as this fel - low ev - er

see, no oth - er fel - low knows her, no -
knew. Her eyes are bright as dia - monds, they

bod - y, on - ly me. She cried so when I left her, it
spark - le like the dew. You may talk a - bout your Dais - y May and

like to broke my heart, and if I ev - er
sing of Ros - a - lee, but the yel - low rose of

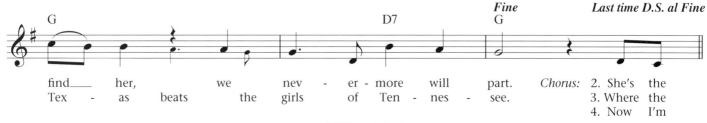

find___ her, we nev - er - more will part. *Chorus:* 2. She's the
Tex - as beats the girls of Ten - nes - see. 3. Where the
4. Now I'm

Additional Lyrics

3. Where the Rio Grande is flowing
and starry nights are bright,
she walks along the river
each quiet summer night.
She thinks of when we parted
so very long ago;
I promised I would come back,
no more to leave her so.
Chorus

4. Now I'm goin' back to find her,
my heart is full of woe.
We'll sing the songs that we used
to sing so long ago.
I'll play the banjo gaily,
we'll sing forever more;
the yellow rose of Texas,
the girl that I adore.
Chorus

Yellow Submarine

Words and Music by JOHN LENNON
and PAUL McCARTNEY

1. In the town_____ where I was born lived a man_____ who sailed the
sailed_____ up to the sun 'til we found_____ the sea of

sea and he told_____ us of his life in the
green. And we lived_____ be - neath the waves in our

1.
land_____ of sub - mar - ines. 2. So we

2.
yel - low sub - mar - ine.

We all live in a ye - low sub - mar - ine, yel - low sub - mar - ine,

yel - low sub - mar - ine. We all live in a yel - low sub - mar - ine,

yel - low sub - mar - ine, yel - low sub - mar - ine. And our friends_____ are all on
As we live_____ a life of

board, man - y more of them live next door. And the band_____ be - gins to
ease, ev - 'ry one of us has all we need: Sky of blue_____ and sea of

1.
play:

2. D.S. and Fade

green in our yel - low sub - mar - ine.

Yes Sir, That's My Baby

Words by
GUS KAHN

Music by
WALTER DONALDSON

You Are My Sunshine

Words and Music by
JIMMIE DAVIS

You Made Me Love You
(I Didn't Want To Do It)

Words by
JOE McCARTHY

Music by
JAMES V. MONACO

Your Cheatin' Heart

Words and Music by
HANK WILLIAMS

You're A Grand Old Flag

Words and Music by
GEORGE M. COHAN

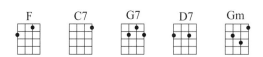

Medium March

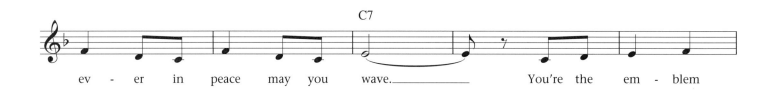

You're a grand old flag, you're a high fly - ing flag, and for -

ev - er in peace may you wave.____ You're the em - blem

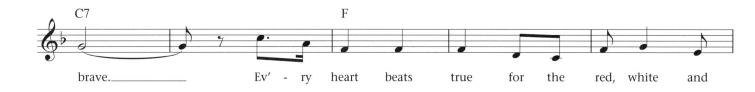

of the land I love, the home of the free and the

brave._____ Ev' - ry heart beats true for the red, white and

blue, where there's nev - er a boast or brag._____

____ But should auld ac - quaint - ance be for -

got keep your eye on the grand old flag._____

You've Got To Hide Your Love Away

Words and Music by JOHN LENNON
and PAUL McCARTNEY

You're Nobody 'Til Somebody Loves You

Words and Music by
RUSS MORGAN, LARRY STOCK
and JAMES CAVANAUGH

284

Songs For
Holidays and Celebrations

Auld Lang Syne

**Words by
ROBERT BURNS**

Traditional Scottish Melody

Should auld ac-quaint-ance be for-got, and nev-er brought to mind? Should

auld ac-quaint - ance be for - got and days of auld lang syne? For

auld_____ lang_____ syne, my dear, for auld_____ lang_____ syne, we'll

take a cup o' kind - ness yet, for auld_____ lang_____ syne.

My Funny Valentine

Words by
LORENZ HART

Music by
RICHARD RODGERS

Too-Ra-Loo-Ra-Loo-Ral
(That's An Irish Melody)

Words and Music by
JAMES R. SHANNON

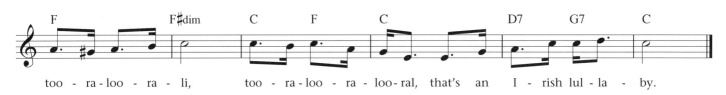

Too - ra - loo - ra - loo - ral, ___ too - ra - loo - ra - li, too - ra - loo - ra -

loo - ral, ___ hush now, don't you cry! ___ Too - ra - loo - ra - loo - ral, ___

too - ra - loo - ra - li, too - ra - loo - ra - loo - ral, that's an I - rish lul - la - by.

When Irish Eyes Are Smiling

Words by CHAUNCEY OLCOTT
and GEORGE GRAFF, JR.

Music by
ERNEST R. BALL

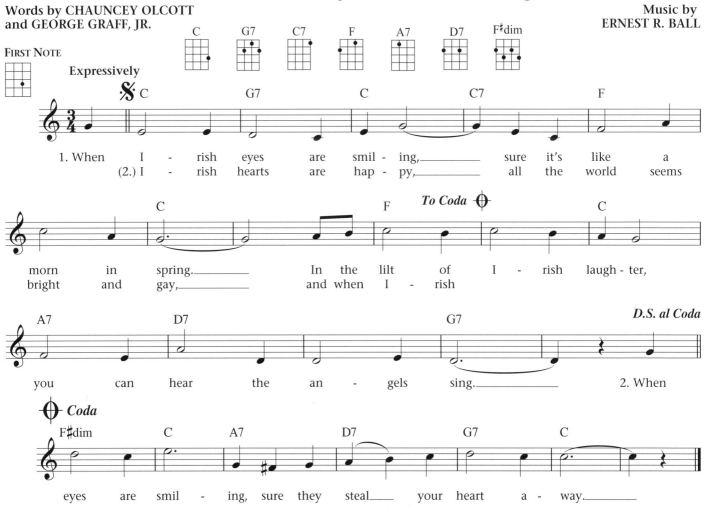

288

Easter Parade

Words and Music by
IRVING BERLIN

Moderately

1. In your East - er bon - net, with all the frills up - on it, you'll
2. I'll be all in clov - er and when they look you o - ver, I'll
3. I could write a son - net a - bout your East - er bon - net, and

be the grand - est la - dy in the East - er Pa - rade.
be the proud - est fel - low in the
of the girl I'm tak - ing to the
East - er Pa -
East - er Pa -

Fine

rade. On the Av - e - nue, Fifth Av - e - nue, the pho
rade.

D.C. (2nd ending) al Fine

to - graph - ers will snap us, and you'll find that you're in the ro - to - gra - vure. Oh,

Anniversary Song

Words and Music by
AL JOLSON and SAUL CHAPLIN

Pomp And Circumstance
(The Graduation Song)

Words by
ARTHUR BENSON

Music by
EDWARD ELGAR

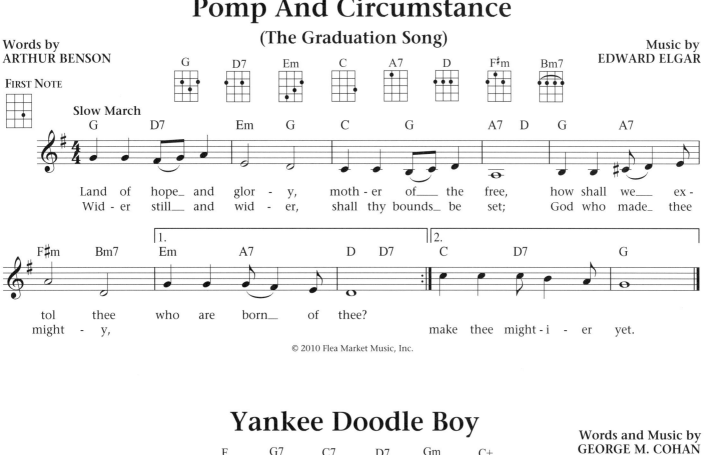

Land of hope_ and glor - y, moth - er of__ the free, how shall we__ ex -
Wid - er still__ and wid - er, shall thy bounds_ be set; God who made_ thee

tol thee who are born__ of thee?
might - y,
make thee might - i - er yet.

Yankee Doodle Boy

Words and Music by
GEORGE M. COHAN

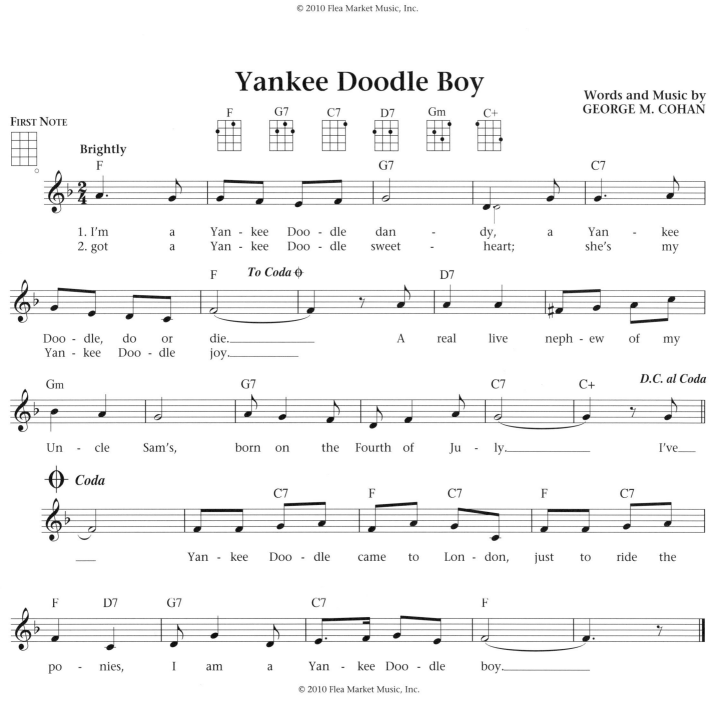

1. I'm a Yan - kee Doo - dle dan - dy, a Yan - kee
2. got a Yan - kee Doo - dle sweet - heart; she's my

Doo - dle, do or die.____ A real live neph - ew of my
Yan - kee Doo - dle joy.____

Un - cle Sam's, born on the Fourth of Ju - ly.____ I've

Yan - kee Doo - dle came to Lon - don, just to ride the

po - nies, I am a Yan - kee Doo - dle boy.____

Over The River And Through The Woods

Words by
LYDIA MARIA CHILD

Traditional

FIRST NOTE

Lively

O - ver the riv - er and through the woods to grand - moth - er's house we go._____ The horse knows the way to car - ry the sleigh through the white and drift - ed snow._____ O - ver the riv - er and through the woods, oh, how the wind does blow!_____ It stings the toes and bites the nose, as o - ver the ground we go._____

Additional Lyrics

2. Over the river and through the woods
to have a first-rate play.
Oh, hear the bells ring: "ting-a-ling ling."
Hurrah for Thanksgiving Day.
Over the river and through the woods,
trot fast, my dapple gray.
Spring o'er the ground like hunting hound,
for this is Thanksgiving Day!

3. Over the river and through the woods,
and straight through the barnyard gate.
We seem to go extremely slow,
it is so hard to wait.
Over the river and through the woods,
now grandmother's cap I spy.
Hurrah for fun, the pudding's done!
Hurrah for the pumpkin pie!

Prayer Of Thanksgiving

Traditional

FIRST NOTE

With Reverence

1. We gath - er to - geth - er to ask the Lord's bless - ing, He
2. Be - side us to guide us, our God with us join - ing, or -
3. We all do ex - tol thee, thou lead - er in bat - tle, and

chas - tens and has - tens His will to make known. The
dain - ing, main - tain - ing His King - dom di - vine. So,
pray that thou still our de - fend - er will be. Let

wick - ed op - press - ing cease them_____ from dis - tress - ing, sing
from the be - gin - ning, the fight_____ we were win - ning, the
thy con - gre - ga - tion es - cape_____ trib - u - la - tion, thy

prais - es to His name, He for - gets not His own.
Lord, is at our side, the glo - ry di - vine.
name be ev - er praised! O, Lord make_____ us free.

The Dreidel Song

Words by
SAMUEL S. GROSSMAN

Music by MIKHL GELBART
and SAMUEL GOLDFARB

Hava Nagila

Hebrew Folk Song

Translation

Let us rejoice, let us rejoice, let us rejoice and be glad.
Let us sing, let us sing, let us sing, and be glad.
Awake, awake brethren, awake with a happy heart.

Away In A Manger

Traditional

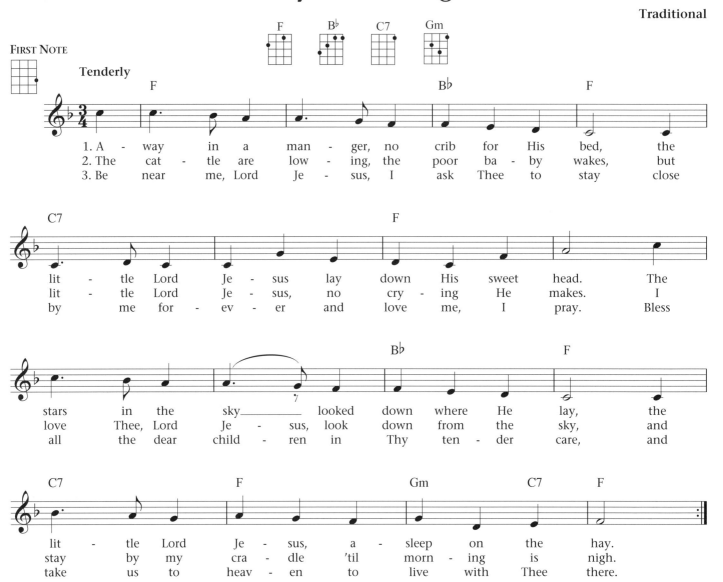

1. A - way in a man - ger, no crib for His bed, the
2. The cat - tle are low - ing, the poor ba - by wakes, but
3. Be near me, Lord Je - sus, I ask Thee to stay close

lit - tle Lord Je - sus lay down His sweet head. The
lit - tle Lord Je - sus, no cry - ing He makes. I
by me for - ev - er and love me, I pray. Bless

stars in the sky_____ looked down where He lay, the
love Thee, Lord Je - sus, look down from the sky, and
all the dear child - ren in Thy ten - der care, and

lit - tle Lord Je - sus, a - sleep on the hay.
stay by my cra - dle 'til morn - ing is nigh.
take us to heav - en to live with Thee there.

Blue Christmas

Words and Music by BILLY HAYES
and JAY JOHNSON

Moderately

I'll have a blue Christ-mas, with-out you._____ I'll be so blue
blue Christ-mas, that's cer - tain._____ And when that blue

think - ing a - bout you._____ Dec - o - ra - tions of red on a
heart -ache starts hurt - in',_____ you'll be do - in' all right with your

1.
green Christ-mas tree won't mean a thing if you're not here with
Christ - mas of

2.
me. I'll have a white, but I'll have a blue, blue Christ - mas_____

The Chipmunk Song

Words and Music by
ROSS BAGDASARIAN

Christ - mas, Christ - mas time is near, time for toys and time for cheer. We've been good but we can't last, hur - ry Christ - mas, hur - ry fast! Want a plane that loops the loop; me, I want a hu - la hoop. We can hard - ly stand the wait, please Christ - mas, don't be late.

Deck The Halls

Traditional Welsh Carol

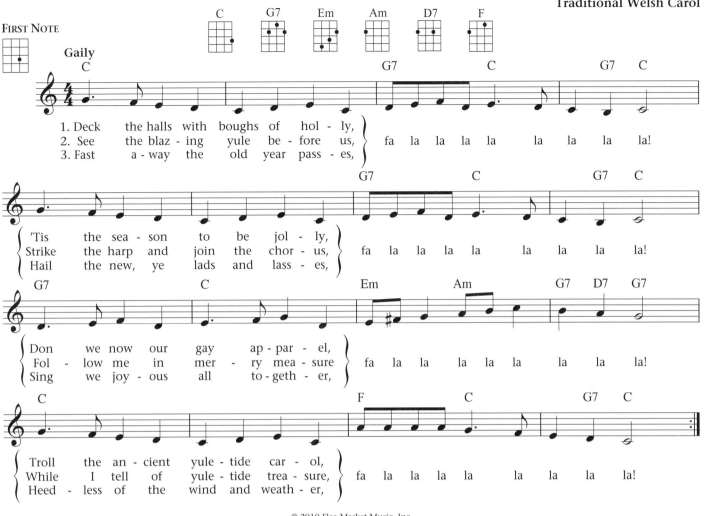

1. Deck the halls with boughs of hol - ly,
2. See the blaz - ing yule be - fore us,
3. Fast a - way the old year pass - es,
fa la la la la la la la la!

'Tis the sea - son to be jol - ly,
Strike the harp and join the chor - us,
Hail the new, ye lads and lass - es,
fa la la la la la la la la!

Don we now our gay ap - par - el,
Fol - low me in mer - ry mea - sure,
Sing we joy - ous all to - geth - er,
fa la la la la la la la la!

Troll the an - cient yule - tide car - ol,
While I tell of yule - tide trea - sure,
Heed - less of the wind and weath - er,
fa la la la la la la la la!

Go Tell It On The Mountain

African-American Spiritual

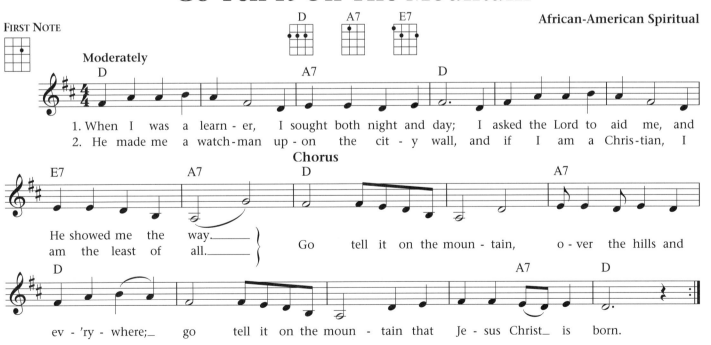

1. When I was a learn - er, I sought both night and day; I asked the Lord to aid me, and
2. He made me a watch - man up - on the cit - y wall, and if I am a Chris - tian, I

Chorus

He showed me the way.___
am the least of all.___
Go tell it on the moun - tain, o - ver the hills and

ev - 'ry - where;___ go tell it on the moun - tain that Je - sus Christ___ is born.

Additional Lyrics

3. While shepherds kept their watching,
   o'er wand'ring flock by night…
   Behold! From out the Heavens,
   there shown a holy light.
   Chorus

4. And lo, when they had seen it,
   they all bowed down and prayed.
   Then they travelled on together,
   to where the Babe was laid.
   Chorus

Feliz Navidad

Words and Music by
JOSÉ FELICIANO

The First Noel

17th Century English Carol

Additional Lyrics

3. And by the light of that same star,
   three wise men came from country far;
   to seek for a King was their intent,
   and to follow the star wherever it went.
   (Chorus)

Hark! The Herald Angels Sing

Words by
CHARLES WESLEY

Music by
FELIX MENDELSSOHN

1. Hark! The her - ald an - gels sing__ "Glo - ry to the new - born king: Peace on earth and
2. Christ, by high - est heav'n a - dored;_ Christ, the ev - er - last - ing Lord! Late in time be -

mer - cy mild,__ God and sin - ners rec - on - ciled!" Joy - ful all ye na - tions, rise,__
hold Him come,_ off - spring of the Vir - gin's womb; veiled in flesh the God - head see,__

join the tri - umph of the skies;__ with the an - gel - ic host pro - claim, "Christ is__ born in
hail the in - car - nate de - i - ty,__ pleased as man with men to dwell, Je - sus__ our Em -

Beth - le - hem!" }
man - u - el. } Hark! The her - ald an - gels sing: "Glo - ry__ to the new - born King."

Joy To The World

Words by
ISAAC WATTS

Music by
GEORGE FRIDERIC HANDEL
Adapted by LOWELL MASON

With Spirit

1. Joy to the world! The Lord has
2. Joy to the world! The Sav - ior

come; let earth re - ceive her King. Let
reigns; let men their songs em - ploy. While

ev - 'ry heart pre - pare Him
fields and floods, rocks, hills and

room, and heav - en and na - ture sing, and
plains re - peat the sound - ing joy, re -

heav - en and na - ture sing, and heav - en and
peat the sound - ing joy, re - peat, re -

heav - en and na - ture sing.
peat the sound - ing joy.

Additional Lyrics

3. No more let sins and sorrows grow,
   nor thorns infest the ground.
   He comes to make His blessings flow
   far as the curse is found.
   Far as the curse is found,
   far as, far as the curse is found.

4. He rules the world with truth and grace,
   and makes the nations prove
   the glories of His righteousness
   and wonders of His love.
   And wonders of His love,
   and wonders, wonders of His love.

Jingle-Bell Rock

Words and Music by
JOE BEAL and JIM BOOTHE

Jingle Bells

Words and Music by
JAMES PIERPONT

1. Dash-ing through the snow in a one-horse o-pen sleigh,
2. Day or two a-go I thought I'd take a ride, and

o'er the fields we go, laugh-ing all the way;
soon Miss Fan-nie Bright was seat-ed by my side; the

bells on bob-tail ring, mak-ing spir-its bright; what
horse was lean and lank, mis-for-tune seemed his lot, he

Chorus

fun it is to ride and sing a sleigh-ing song to-night! } Oh, Jin-gle bells! Jin-gle bells!
got in-to a drift-ed bank and we, we got up-sot.

Jin-gle all the way! Oh, what fun it is to ride in a

one-horse o-pen sleigh!___ Jin-gle bells! Jin-gle bells! Jin-gle all the way!

Oh, what fun it is to ride in a one-horse o-pen sleigh!

Additional Lyrics

3. Now the ground is white,
go it while you're young.
Take the girls tonight,
and sing this sleighing song.
Just get a bobtailed nag,
two-forty for his speed.
Then hitch him to an open sleigh,
and crack you'll take the lead.
Chorus

Let It Snow! Let It Snow! Let It Snow!

Words by
SAMMY CAHN

Music by
JULE STYNE

1. Oh the weath-er out - side is fright - ful, but the fire is so de -
(2.) does - n't show signs of stop - ping, and I brought some corn for
(3.) fire is slow - ly dy - ing, and, my dear, we're still good -

light - ful. And since we've no place to go, let it
pop - ping. The lights are turned way down low,
bye - ing. But as long as you love me so,

snow! Let it snow! Let it snow! 2. It snow! When we snow!

fi - nal-ly kiss good - night, how I'll hate go - ing out in the storm! But if

you'll real - ly hold me tight, all the way home I'll be warm. 3. The

Mele Kalikimaka

Words and Music by
R. ALEX ANDERSON

Me - le Ka - li - ki - ma - ka is the thing to say ____ on a bright Ha -

wai - ian Christ - mas day. ____ That's the Is - land greet - ing that we send to you, _

_ from the land where palm trees sway. ____ Here we know that

Christ - mas will be green and bright, the sun will shine by day, and all the

stars at night. Me - le Ka - li - ki - ma - ka is Ha - wai - i's

way to say Mer - ry Christ - mas to you. ____

O Come, All Ye Faithful
(Adeste Fideles)

Latin Words Translated by
FREDERICK OAKELEY

Music by
JOHN FRANCIS WADE

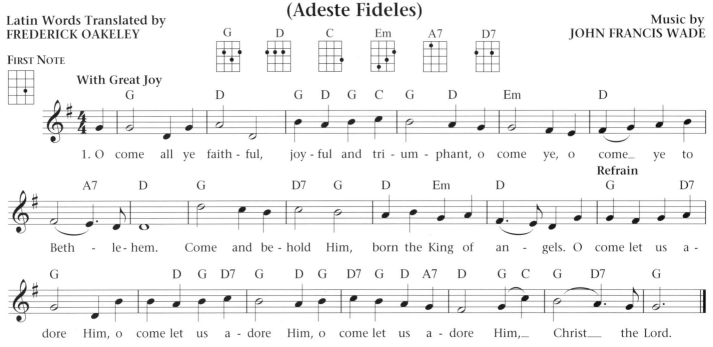

1. O come all ye faith-ful, joy-ful and tri-um-phant, o come ye, o come ye to Beth-le-hem. Come and be-hold Him, born the King of an-gels. O come let us a-dore Him, o come let us a-dore Him, o come let us a-dore Him,__ Christ__ the Lord.

Additional Lyrics

2. Sing, choirs of angels,
   sing in exultation,
   sing, all ye citizens of heaven above:
   Glory to God,
   glory in the highest!
   Refrain

3. Yes, Lord, we greet thee,
   born this happy morning,
   Jesus, to Thee be glory given.
   Word of the Father,
   now in flesh appearing.
   Refrain

Silent Night

Words by **JOSEPH MÖHR**
Translated by **JOHN F. YOUNG**

Music by
FRANZ X. GRUBER

1. Si - lent night, ho - ly night, all is calm, all is bright,
2. Si - lent night, ho - ly night, shep - herds quake at the sight.

'round yon Vir - gin Moth - er and child, Ho - ly In - fant so ten - der and
Glo - ries stream__ from heav - en a - far, heav'n - ly hosts__ sing Al - le - lu -

mild, sleep in heav - en - ly peace.____ Sleep__ in heav - en - ly peace.____
ia; Christ the Sav - ior is born.____ Christ__ the Sav - ior is born.____

3. Silent night, Holy night,
   Son of God, love's pure light.
   Radiant beams from thy holy face,
   with the dawn of redeeming grace,
   Jesus, Lord at thy birth.
   Jesus, Lord at thy birth.

Rudolph The Red-Nosed Reindeer

Words and Music by
JOHNNY MARKS

We Three Kings Of Orient Are

Words and Music by
JOHN H. HOPKINS, JR.

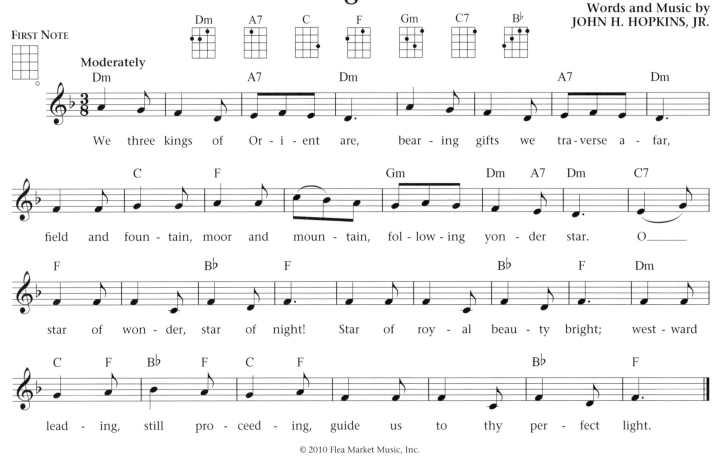

© 2010 Flea Market Music, Inc.

We Wish You A Merry Christmas

Traditional
English Folksong

© 2010 Flea Market Music, Inc.

Songs For Children

All Night, All Day

Spiritual

All night, all day, an-gels watch-in' o-ver me, my Lord.

All night, all day, an-gels watch-in' o-ver me.

1. Now I lay me down to sleep, an-gels watch-in' o-ver me, my
2. If I die be-fore I wake, an-gels watch-in' o-ver me, my

Lord. Pray the Lord my soul to keep, an-gels watch-in' o-ver me.
Lord. Pray the Lord my soul to take, an-gels watch-in' o-ver me.

All Through The Night

Welsh Folksong

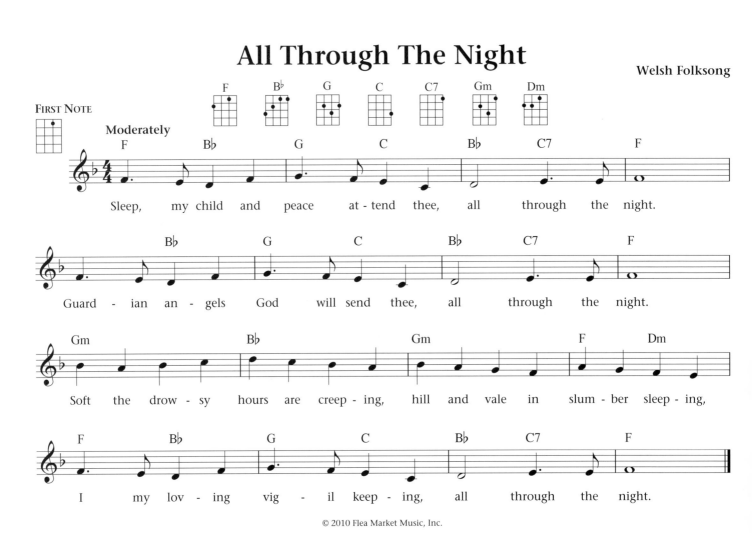

Sleep, my child and peace at-tend thee, all through the night.

Guard-ian an-gels God will send thee, all through the night.

Soft the drow-sy hours are creep-ing, hill and vale in slum-ber sleep-ing,

I my lov-ing vig-il keep-ing, all through the night.

Alphabet Song

Traditional

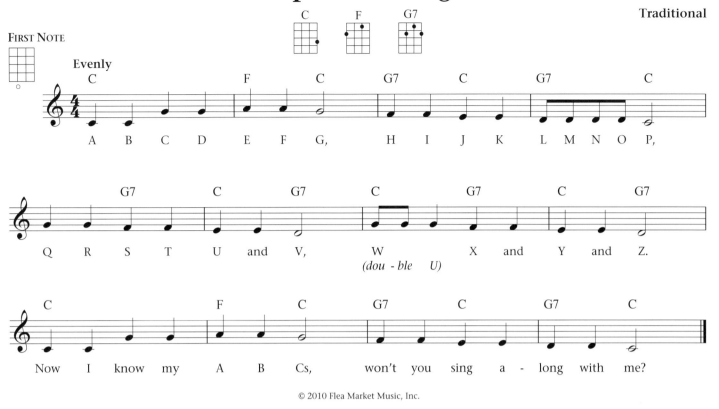

Baa, Baa, Black Sheep

Traditional

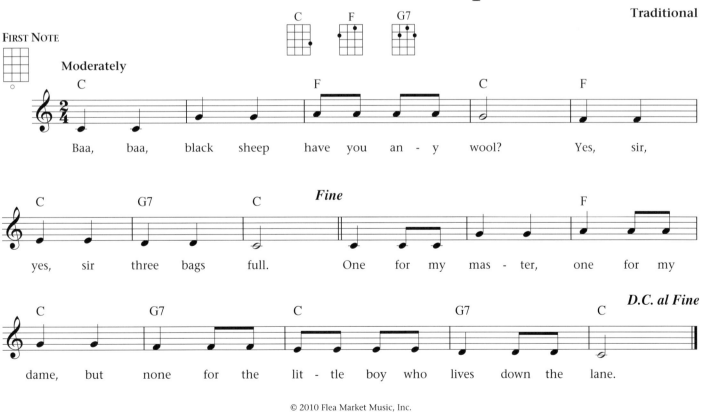

The Bear Went Over The Mountain

Traditional

The bear went o - ver the moun - tain, the bear went o - ver the moun - tain, the bear went o - ver the moun - tain to see what he could see.

To see what he could
He saw the oth - er

see,___ and all that he could see was the
side,___ he saw the oth - er side. He saw the

oth - er side of the moun - tain, the

D.C. al Fine

oth - er side of the moun - tain, the oth - er side of the moun - tain was all that he could see.

Brahms' Lullaby

Words by
KARL SIMROCK

Music by
JOHANNES BRAHMS

1. Lull - a - by and good - night, with___ ros - es be - dight,___ with___
2. Lull - a - by and good - night, thy___ moth - er's de - light.___ Bright_

li - lies o'er___ spread, is___ ba - by's wee bed. Lay thee
an - gels be - side my___ darl - ing a - bide. They will

down now and rest, may thy slum - ber be blessed. Lay thee
guard thee at rest, thou shalt wake on my breast. They will

down now and rest, may thy slum - ber be blessed.
guard thee at rest, thou shalt wake on my breast.

The Candy Man

Words and Music by
LESLIE BRICUSSE and
ANTHONY NEWLEY

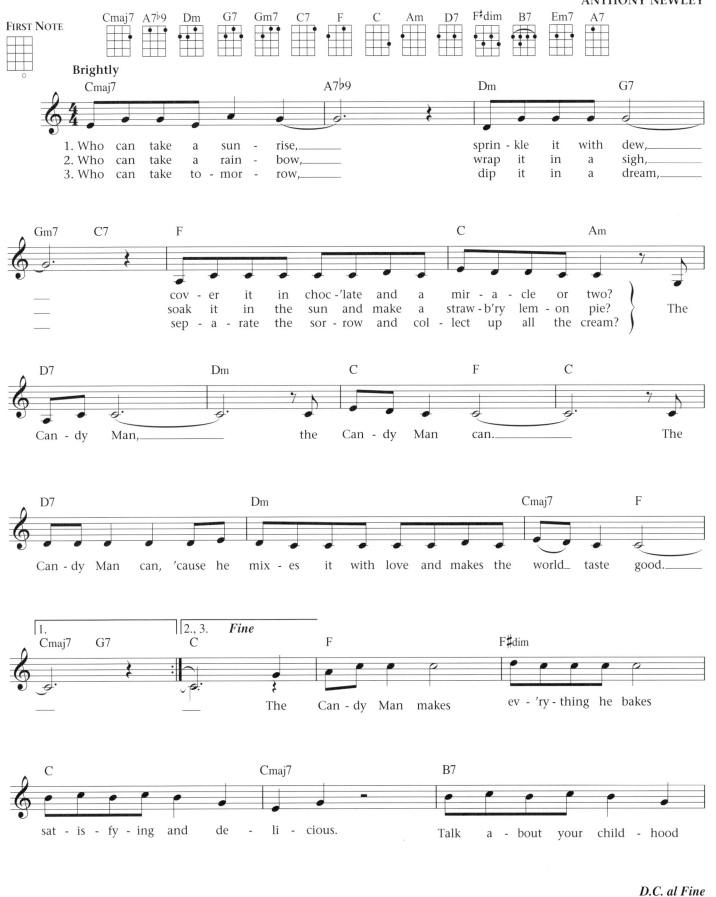

Do-Re-Mi

Lyrics by
OSCAR HAMMERSTEIN II

Music by
RICHARD RODGERS

Eensy Weensy Spider

Traditional

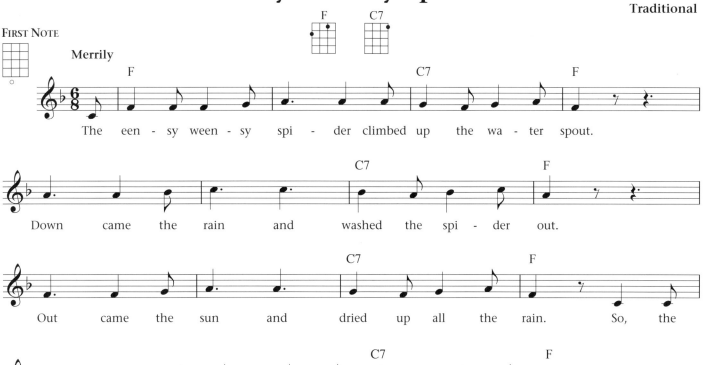

The een-sy ween-sy spi-der climbed up the wa-ter spout.

Down came the rain and washed the spi-der out.

Out came the sun and dried up all the rain. So, the

een-sy ween-sy spi-der climbed up the spout a-gain.

The Farmer In The Dell

Traditional

1. The farm-er in the dell,_____ the farm-er in the dell:
2. The farm-er takes a wife,_____ the farm-er takes a wife:
3. *(See additional lyrics)*

Heigh - ho, the der-ry-o! { The farm-er in the dell.
                           { The farm-er takes a wife.

Additional Lyrics

3. The wife takes a child,
the wife takes a child:
Heigh-ho, the derry-o!
The wife takes a child.

4. The child takes a nurse,
the child takes a nurse:
Heigh-ho, the derry-o!
The child takes a nurse.

5. The nurse takes a cow,
the nurse takes a cow:
Heigh-ho, the derry-o!
The nurse takes a cow.

6. The cow takes a dog,
the cow takes a dog:
Heigh-ho, the derry-o!
The cow takes a dog.

7. The dog takes a cat,
the dog takes a cat:
Heigh-ho, the derry-o!
The dog takes a cat.

8. The cat takes a rat,
the cat takes a rat:
Heigh-ho, the derry-o!
The cat takes a rat.

9. The rat takes the cheese,
the rat takes the cheese:
Heigh-ho, the derry-o!
The rat takes the cheese.

10. The cheese stands alone,
the cheese stands alone:
Heigh-ho, the derry-o!
The cheese stands alone.

Hush, Little Baby

Folk Lullaby

1. Hush, lit - tle ba - by, don't say a word, Pa - pa's gon - na buy you a
2. And if that dia - mond ring turns brass, Pa - pa's gon - na buy you a
3. And if that bil - ly goat won't pull, Pa - pa's gon - na buy you a
4. And if that dog named Rover don't bark, Pa - pa's gon - na buy you a

mock - ing - bird. And if that mock - ing - bird don't sing,
look - ing - glass. And if that look - ing - glass gets broke,
cart and bull. And if that cart and bull turn over,
horse and cart. And if that horse and cart fall down,

Pa - pa's gon - na buy you a dia - mond ring.
Pa - pa's gon - na buy you a bil - ly goat.
Pa - pa's gon - na buy you a dog named Rover.
you'll still be the sweet - est ba - by in town.

If You're Happy And You Know It

Traditional

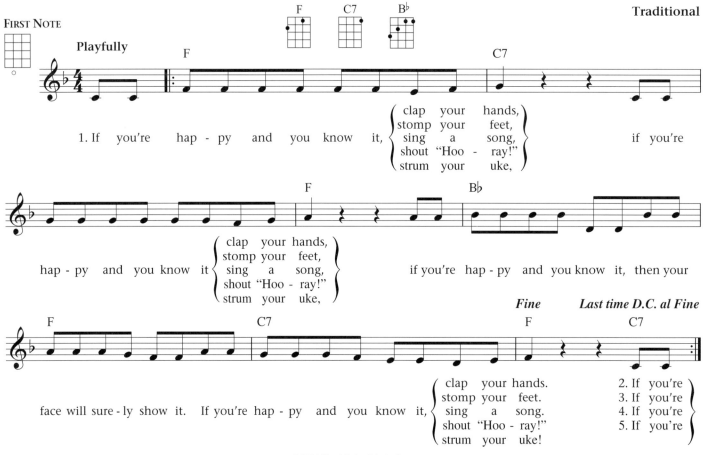

1. If you're hap - py and you know it,
{ clap your hands,
stomp your feet,
sing a song,
shout "Hoo - ray!"
strum your uke, }
if you're

hap - py and you know it
{ clap your hands,
stomp your feet,
sing a song,
shout "Hoo - ray!"
strum your uke, }
if you're hap - py and you know it, then your

Fine   *Last time D.C. al Fine*

face will sure - ly show it. If you're hap - py and you know it,
{ clap your hands.
stomp your feet.
sing a song.
shout "Hoo - ray!"
strum your uke! }
2. If you're
3. If you're
4. If you're
5. If you're

Good Morning To All
(Happy Birthday)

Words by
PATTY S. HILL

Music by
MILDRED J. HILL

It's A Small World

From "It's a Small World" at Disneyland Park and Magic Kingdom Park

Words and Music by
RICHARD M. SHERMAN
and ROBERT B. SHERMAN

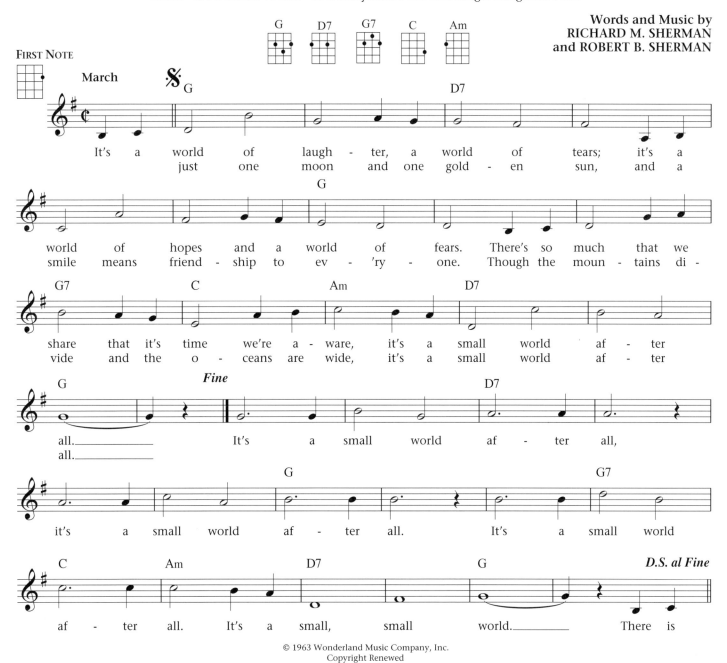

Mary Had A Little Lamb

Children's Song

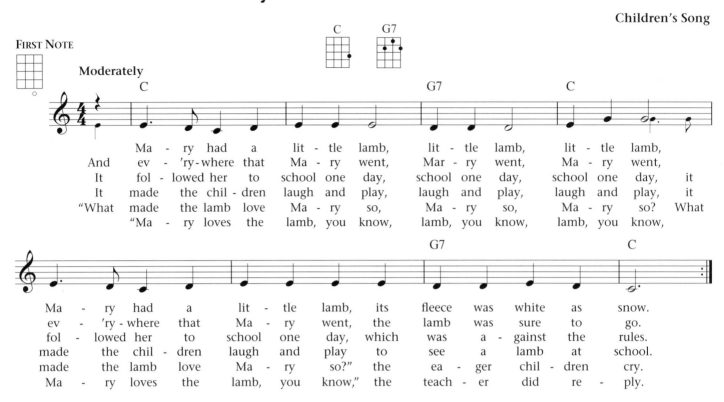

Ma - ry had a lit - tle lamb, lit - tle lamb, lit - tle lamb,
And ev - 'ry-where that Ma - ry went, Mar - ry went, Ma - ry went,
It fol - lowed her to school one day, school one day, school one day, it
It made the chil - dren laugh and play, laugh and play, laugh and play, it
"What made the lamb love Ma - ry so, Ma - ry so, Ma - ry so? What
"Ma - ry loves the lamb, you know, lamb, you know, lamb, you know,

Ma - ry had a lit - tle lamb, its fleece was white as snow.
ev - 'ry - where that Ma - ry went, the lamb was sure to go.
fol - lowed her to school one day, which was a - gainst the rules.
made the chil - dren laugh and play to see a lamb at school.
made the lamb love Ma - ry so?" the ea - ger chil - dren cry.
Ma - ry loves the lamb, you know," the teach - er did re - ply.

The More We Get Together

New Words by
JIM BELOFF

Traditional

Oh, the more we get to - geth - er, to - geth - er, to - geth - er, the more we get to -
Oh, let's play the u - ku - le - le, let's all play it dai - ly, the more we play it

geth - er, the hap - pier we'll be. For your friends are my friends and my friends are
dai - ly, the hap - pier we'll be! When I uke and you uke and we uke and

your friends. Oh, the more we get to - geth - er, the hap - pier we'll be.
they uke, yes the more we play it dai - ly, the hap - pier we'll be!

Mickey Mouse March

Words and Music by
JIMMIE DODD

Mick - ey Mouse Club! Mick - ey Mouse Club!
1. Who's the lead - er
2. Hey, there, hi, there!
3. Come a - long and

of the club that's made for you and me?
Ho, there! You're as wel - come as can be!
sing a song and join the jam - bo - ree!

M - I - C - K - E - Y

M - O - U - S - E!

E! Mick - ey Mouse!

Mick - ey Mouse!

For-

ev - er let us hold our ban - ner high! (High! High! High!)

E!

Oh Where, Oh Where
Has My Little Dog Gone?

Words by SEP. WINNER

Traditional Melody

Oh where, oh where has my lit - tle dog gone! Oh where, oh

where can he be?_____ With his ears cut short and his

tail cut long, oh where, oh where can he be?_____

On The Good Ship Lollipop

Words and Music by
SIDNEY CLARE and
RICHARD A. WHITING

Old MacDonald Had A Farm

Traditional

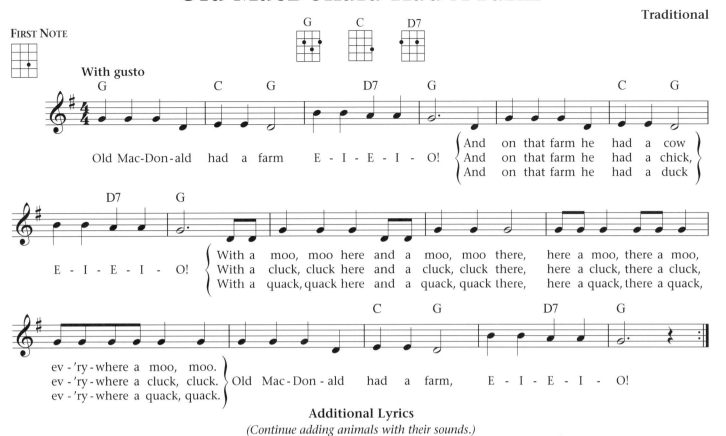

{ And on that farm he had a cow }
{ And on that farm he had a chick, }
{ And on that farm he had a duck }

{ With a moo, moo here and a moo, moo there, here a moo, there a moo, }
{ With a cluck, cluck here and a cluck, cluck there, here a cluck, there a cluck, }
{ With a quack, quack here and a quack, quack there, here a quack, there a quack, }

ev-'ry-where a moo, moo.
ev-'ry-where a cluck, cluck. } Old Mac-Don-ald had a farm, E-I-E-I-O!
ev-'ry-where a quack, quack.

Additional Lyrics
(Continue adding animals with their sounds.)

4. Pig—oink, oink; 5. Cat—meow, meow; 6. Horse—neigh, neigh; 7. Dog—woof, woof; 8. Turkey—gobble, gobble

Polly Wolly Doodle

Traditional American Minstrel Song

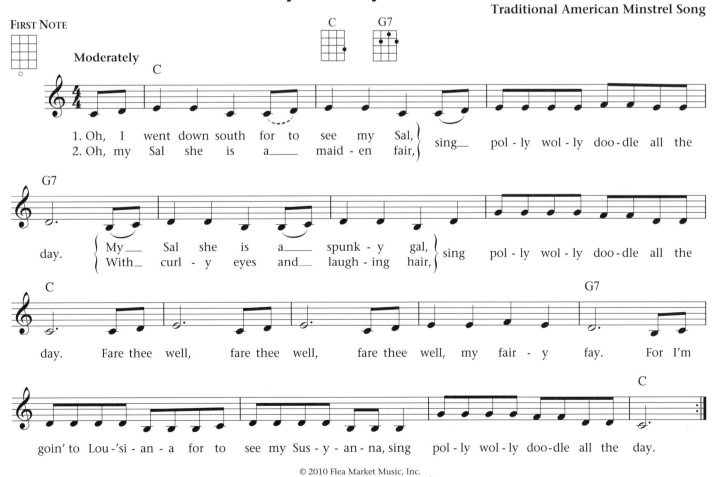

The Rainbow Connection

Words and Music by
PAUL WILLIAMS and
KENNETH L. ASCHER

Row, Row, Row Your Boat

Traditional

Skip To My Lou

Traditional

A Spoonful Of Sugar

Words and Music by
RICHARD M. SHERMAN
and ROBERT B. SHERMAN

Supercalifragilisticexpialidocious

Words and Music by
RICHARD M. SHERMAN and
ROBERT B. SHERMAN

This Old Man

Traditional

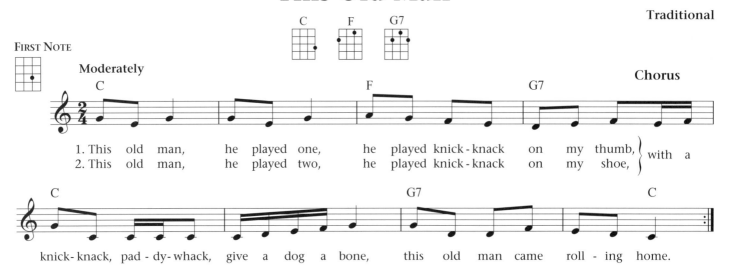

FIRST NOTE

Moderately

Chorus

1. This old man, he played one, he played knick-knack on my thumb, } with a
2. This old man, he played two, he played knick-knack on my shoe, } with a

knick-knack, pad-dy-whack, give a dog a bone, this old man came roll-ing home.

Additional Lyrics

3. This old man, he played three,
   he played knick-knack on my knee.
   Chorus

4. This old man, he played four,
   he played knick-knack on my door.
   Chorus

5. This old man, he played five,
   he played knick-knack on my hive.
   Chorus

6. This old man, he played six,
   he played knick-knack on my sticks.
   Chorus

7. This old man, he played seven,
   he played knick-knack up to heaven.
   Chorus

8. This old man, he played eight,
   he played knick-knack on my gate.
   Chorus

9. This old man, he played nine,
   he played knick-knack on my vine.
   Chorus

10. This old man, he played ten,
    he played knick-knack over again.
    Chorus

Three Blind Mice

Traditional

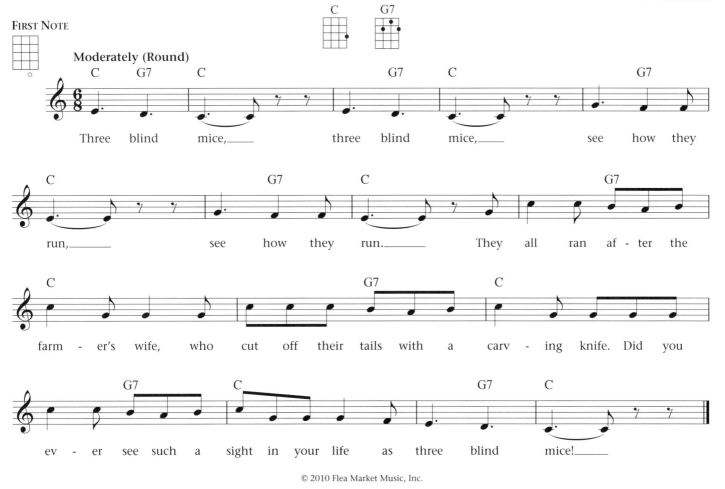

Three blind mice, three blind mice, see how they run, see how they run. They all ran af-ter the farm-er's wife, who cut off their tails with a carv-ing knife. Did you ev-er see such a sight in your life as three blind mice!

Upside Down

Words and Music by
JACK JOHNSON

Bb ... C ... F

I don't want this feel - in' to go a - way.

Coda

Bb ... C ... Am ... Gm

This world keeps spin - nin' and there's no time to waste. Well, it

Am ... Bb ... C ... F ... Gm

all keeps spin - nin', spin - nin' 'round and 'round and up - side down.

Bb ... C ... F ... Gm ... Bb ... C

Who's to say what's im - pos - si - ble and can't be found? I don't want this feel - in' to go a -

F ... Gm ... F

way. Please don't go a - way.

Twinkle, Twinkle Little Star

Traditional

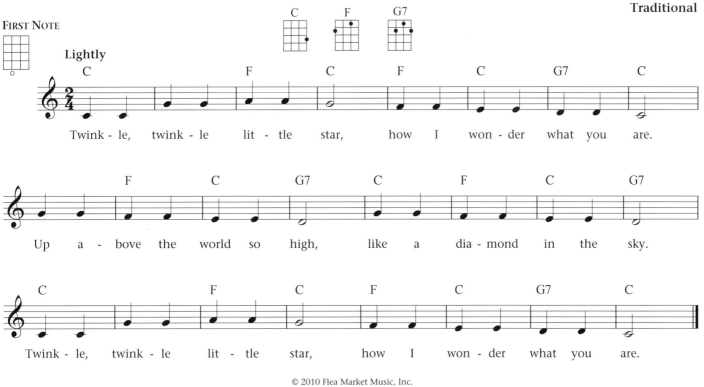

FIRST NOTE

Lightly

C ... F ... C ... F ... C ... G7 ... C

Twink - le, twink - le lit - tle star, how I won - der what you are.

F ... C ... G7 ... C ... F ... C ... G7

Up a - bove the world so high, like a dia - mond in the sky.

C ... F ... C ... F ... C ... G7 ... C

Twink - le, twink - le lit - tle star, how I won - der what you are.

You've Got A Friend In Me

Words and Music by
RANDY NEWMAN

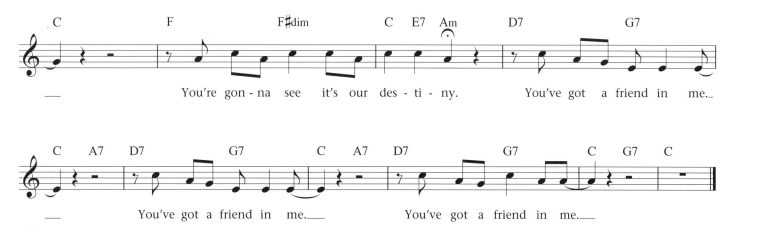

Zip-A-Dee-Doo-Dah

**Words by
RAY GILBERT**

**Music by
ALLIE WRUBEL**

Your Notes Here

Your Notes Here

Thank You

Our biggest thank you goes to Ronny Schiff and Charylu Roberts, both of whom have been part of the team since the very first Jumpin' Jim's songbook. Also, major thanks to Jeff Schroedl, Dan Bauer, Jerry Muccio, David Jahnke, David Dinan, Denis Kavemeier, Trish Dulka, Lori Hagopian, Larry Morton, Keith Mardak and everyone else at Hal Leonard Corp. for your enormous help in making this songbook a reality. Finally, thank you to all who suggested songs or helped in one way or another to make this book what it is, especially: Tony Cappa, Andy Andrews, Peter Thomas, Pete McDonnell, Rick Scanlan, Geoff Rezek, Mike and Marv Beloff, Liz Drouin, Eileen Schiess, Jim Rosokoff, John and Evelyn Chandler, Lionel Cranfield, Fred Sokolow, Phil Rosenthal, Tim Mann, Lil' Rev, Pete Zaccagnino, Shirley Davis, Shirley Orlando, Susan McCormick, Paul Cundari, Doug Haverty, and Steve Boisen. And you!

Liz and Jim Beloff

Finding a ukulele at the Pasadena Rose Bowl Flea Market in 1992 inspired Liz and Jim Beloff to start Flea Market Music, Inc., publisher of the popular *Jumpin' Jim's* series of ukulele songbooks. This series is sold worldwide and includes *The Daily Ukulele: 365 Songs For Better Living* and *The Daily Ukulele: Leap Year Edition*, two of the biggest and best-selling ukulele songbooks ever published.

Rick Scanlan Photography

Jim Beloff is the author of *The Ukulele—A Visual History* (Backbeat Books), producer of *Legends of Ukulele*, a CD compilation for Rhino Records and has made three how-to-play DVDs for Homespun Tapes. Jim is also an active songwriter. His two-CD set, *Dreams I Left In Pockets*, features 33 songs he wrote or co-wrote with uke legends Herb "Ohta-san" Ohta and Lyle Ritz.

Liz Maihock Beloff, with a background in film and television graphics, designs the covers and art-directs all of FMM's songbooks, CDs and DVDs. She is also a talented singer who, before teaming up with Jim, sang with *a cappella* groups in college and New York City.

As performers, Liz and Jim have become known for their breezy, close harmonies on standards and Jim's original songs. They perform together regularly throughout the USA, playing their family-made *Fluke, Flea* and *Firefly* ukuleles. They have also toured Japan, Australia and Canada and believe in their company's motto, "Uke Can Change the World."
www.fleamarketmusic.com and *facebook.com/jimbeloffmusic*

Also Available:

The Daily Ukulele: Leap Year Edition

The Daily Ukulele: Baritone Edition